MADE YOU LOOK

MADE
YOU LOOK

HOW ADVERTISING WORKS
AND WHY YOU SHOULD KNOW

SHARI GRAYDON

ILLUSTRATED BY
MICHELLE LAMOREAUX

annick press
toronto + new york + vancouver

Revised edition:
Editor: Paula Ayer
Researchers: Jennifer Croll, Stacey Matson
Copyedited by Pam Robertson
Proofread by Linda Pruessen
Designed by Natalie Olsen, Kisscut Design
First edition edited by Pam Robertson

Annick Press Ltd.

We acknowledge the support of the Canada Council for the Arts, the Ontario Arts Council, and the Government of Canada through the Canada Book Fund (CBF) for our publishing activities.

ONTARIO ARTS COUNCIL
CONSEIL DES ARTS DE L'ONTARIO
50 YEARS OF ONTARIO GOVERNMENT SUPPORT OF THE ARTS
50 ANS DE SOUTIEN DU GOUVERNEMENT DE L'ONTARIO AUX ARTS

Cataloging in Publication

Graydon, Shari, 1958–
Made you look : how advertising works and why you should know /
Shari Graydon ; illustrated by Michelle Lamoreaux. — Rev. ed.

Includes bibliographical references and index.
Issued also in electronic formats.
ISBN 978-1-55451-561-5 (bound).—ISBN 978-1-55451-560-8 (pbk.)

1. Advertising—Juvenile literature. I. Lamoreaux, Michelle Ann II. Title.

HF5829.G73 2013   j659.1   C2013-901259-1

Distributed in Canada by:
Firefly Books Ltd.
50 Staples Avenue, Unit 1
Richmond Hill, ON L4B 0A7

Published in the U.S.A. by Annick Press (U.S.) Ltd.
Distributed in the U.S.A. by: Firefly Books (U.S.) Inc.
P.O. Box 1338 Ellicott Station
Buffalo, NY 14205

Printed in China

Visit us at: www.annickpress.com
Visit Shari Graydon at: www.sharigraydon.com
Visit Michelle Lamoreaux at: www.shannonassociates.com/artist/michellelamoreaux

CONTENTS

CHAPTER 1
AD POWER

Do you remember the day your parents sat you down to have a serious talk about advertising?

Me neither. And it's not something they ever test you on at school. Which is too bad: it's so easy to remember jingles and slogans that an ad exam might be the one test all year you wouldn't have to study for!

Really, you've been "studying" the subject almost since the day you were born: even as a baby, every time you got parked in front of the TV or carried past a store sign, you were absorbing the art—or some would say science—of persuasive communication.

You could say that advertising is basically anything someone does to grab your attention and hold onto it long enough to tell you how cool, fast, cheap, tasty, or awesome whatever they're selling is. Some people have a different view of it: they argue that advertising is trickery used to shut down your brain just long enough to convince you to open your wallet!

Whichever way you look at advertising, though, it's so much a part of our world that trying to imagine life without it starts to feel like a science-fiction movie: *Black Holes and Other Mysteries of Life Before Advertising*. And what do you want to bet it would be in black and white?

ADVERTISING IN ANCIENT HISTORY

Advertising has been around in one form or another practically since people began rubbing two sticks together to make fire.

In ancient Greece, people put up posters offering rewards, and painted ads on their houses when they wanted to move.

In ancient Babylonia (now part of Iraq), the names of kings were stenciled on temples and buildings.

As cities developed, merchants carved wooden signs to hang outside their shops. Since most people couldn't read, the signs used pictures, not words.

THE PRINTED WORLD

In the 1400s, the invention of the printing press revolutionized everything. Before then, religious leaders and scholars were generally the only people who could read and write; everyone else had to rely on oral communication—speaking and listening.

But the printing press made books more affordable and gave people more opportunity to become literate. The printing press also made it easy to produce other kinds of printed materials. As a result, handbills (single-sheet brochures) and posters became the first forms of "mass media" (literally, media available to masses of people).

The earliest surviving print advertisement is a handbill that was posted on the door of a London church in 1472.

But many people still couldn't read. It wasn't until 200 years later that the first known newspaper ad—offering a reward for a stolen horse—showed up.

Soon there were newspapers, and then newspaper ads for all sorts of goods, such as coffee, real estate, and medicines. By 1758, there were so many advertisements that Samuel Johnson, a famous British writer, suggested that people had stopped paying attention to them, forcing advertisers to make "magnificent promises" —outrageous claims about what their products could do. (Two and a half centuries later, people are still complaining about advertisers' tendency to exaggerate the truth.)

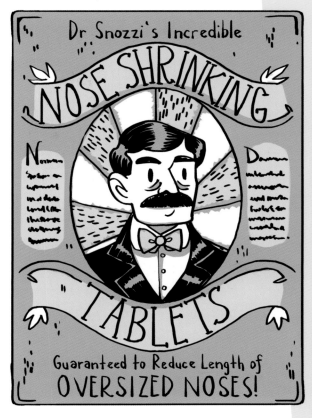

"Patent medicines" came to be seen as the biggest offenders. For one thing, they were rarely real medicine, and for another, their creators usually didn't even bother registering these so-called "miracle cures" with the patent office, which was responsible for recording who invented what.

THE REAL THING

One of the world's best-known products started out more than a century ago as a patent medicine. In the early 1900s, its ads promised users relief from headaches and exhaustion. Today, its claim, to quench your thirst, is more modest. But its name, Coca-Cola, has remained the same.

CREATING CONSUMERS

By *the early 1800s,* the industrial revolution had introduced machine power to manufacturing in Europe and North America. This allowed companies to produce many more goods at a much faster rate. Suddenly, things that people usually had to make themselves—like soap and candles—were now cheaper to buy than to make at home.

You might think that families would have been happy to give up the time-consuming process of churning butter or gathering beeswax. But most people weren't used to buying things. They had to be persuaded to start spending their money on the products companies were making for them.

That's when advertising really jumped into high gear. Its job became not only to get people to buy, but to convince them to think of themselves differently—as consumers. At the time, this was a radical idea. People tended to define themselves by what they did, or made. If they were competitive with their neighbors, it wasn't about who had the newest car or the biggest TV. It was much more about baking a tastier loaf of bread or being more skilled with a handsaw. Folks who had to buy their goods from someone else might actually be considered incompetent!

Advertisers had to work hard to change that attitude, to persuade people that factory-made—as opposed to homemade—items were better. One of the ways advertisers did this was to put logos on their packages. Campbell's Soup and Quaker Oats were among the first to do so, in the 1880s. The logos were designed to make mass-produced goods seem more familiar or personal. Characters— like the man who still appears as part of the Quaker Oats logo— were created to make people feel as if they were buying from a trusted shopkeeper.

WHAT'S A LOGO?

A logo is a company's identifying "signature." It can be simply the company's name, written in a special style (like Coca-Cola's logo, for instance); it can be a symbol (like Nike's "swoosh"); or it can be a combination (like the Domino's Pizza logo, with the company's name next to a red domino).

CHANGING WITH THE TIMES

1400s: The invention of the printing press means ads can be mass produced.

1800s: Railways speed up postal service, leading to more ads sent through the mail.

1839: Photography lets advertisers show images of real people, products, and places, instead of drawings.

1920s: Radio introduces a new world of advertising that goes in one ear and out the other.

THE GOLDEN AGE: RADIO AND TV

When radio was first introduced, many people resisted the idea that commercials should be allowed on the airwaves. In 1922, for example, a senior US government official said it was unthinkable that radio should be "drowned in advertising chatter."

Advertisers themselves weren't immediately enthusiastic either. But as radio became more popular, they became more interested. In fact, the term "soap opera" was coined in the early days of radio, when soap companies "sponsored" radio dramas. This meant that rather than simply promoting their product in a 15- or 30-second commercial, the companies and their ad agencies actually wrote the scripts, hired the actors, and produced the plays—working in mentions of their products in the process.

Television, which was first broadcast in North America in 1939, adopted an approach similar to radio at first. The programs were named after their sponsors, resulting in *Kraft Television Theatre* and *Goodyear TV Playhouse*.

But by the 1950s, the cost of producing television programs was increasing, making it more difficult for a single advertiser to foot the bill. Advertisers were forced to give up control of the programs and instead had to buy the shorter commercial spots that are common today. For decades, advertising on TV has been considered the best way to reach a mass audience—and companies pay big money to run their spots during popular shows.

Darling, I love you.

And I love how CLEEN brand laundry soap gets rid of the toughest stains!

Now, in the 21st century, that strategy is changing. Many television viewers use digital devices to record shows, stream shows online or download them, or watch whenever they want with on-demand services. The problem for advertisers? Some of these ways of consuming television allow viewers to avoid watching ads. Their solution has been to integrate products and promotional messages into the programs themselves—not so different from early radio soap operas! One of the biggest venues for such product placement is also one of the fastest-growing segments of TV: reality television. Companies regularly sponsor reality TV shows, and you'll find their brand-name products throughout, often with "challenges" or even musical numbers built around them.

ADVERTISING GOES DIGITAL

Since the 1990s, advertisers have had a new means of reaching the people they want to influence: the internet. Advertising on the internet works differently from advertising on TV or radio, since it can be much more interactive and targeted to each user. Some advertisers use pop-ups or banner ads at the top of popular websites. Others use keyword-based advertising in search engines like Google, which shows you ads related to what you're looking for. Still others create their own flashy sites, sometimes with games or contests, to attract users to visit and buy online. Companies also use social media sites to engage web users one-on-one and create positive buzz around their brands. The digital world changes quickly, so advertisers are always experimenting to find the most effective ways to promote their products and services online.

Communications technology continues to evolve. Digital streaming devices are replacing DVD players, video games are becoming more realistic all the time, and smartphones allow us to take our TV and internet with us wherever we go. Can you imagine what options there might be 10 or 15 years from *now?*

ADS UNLIMITED

There's an old saying that can be applied to today's ad-filled world: *To the fish, the water is invisible.* In other words, when you're surrounded by something all the time, you don't notice it. You take it for granted and assume that it's natural, or that it's always been there. You don't think about whether it's good or bad, or how it's affecting your life.

In parts of the world where people have a lot of modern conveniences and up-to-date technology, you could say that advertising has become "the water in which we swim." There's so much of it that we hardly notice it anymore. In fact, some experts estimate that a young person growing up in North America may see up to 40,000 TV commercials every year. When you add in all the advertisements from other media— magazines, billboards, games, the internet— it's easy to see how you'd begin to stop noticing, and just keep swimming.

ADDING UP ADS

Most people agree there's a lot of advertising around us, but how much, exactly? Some say the average person is exposed to several thousand ads every day, while others claim it's more like a couple hundred—or fewer if you only count the ads people really pay attention to. As an experiment, try counting all the ads you see in one day. If you try this, don't forget to include:

FAN PAGES ON FACEBOOK

FRIDGE MAGNETS

RADIO JINGLES

PROMOTIONAL MESSAGES ON YOUR MORNING CEREAL BOX

ADVERTISING TEXT MESSAGES ON MOBILE PHONES

SPONSORED TWEETS ON TWITTER

OUTDOOR BILLBOARDS

THE NEON AND AWNING SIGNS OF LOCAL STORES

POSTERS ON TELEPHONE POLES

POSTERS IN SCHOOL HALLWAYS

ADS THAT SHOW UP WHEN YOU SEARCH THE WEB

LOGOS ON YOUR FRIENDS' CLOTHES

ADS IN MAGAZINES

ADS ON CITY BUSES

BUMPER STICKERS

COMMERCIALS ON TV

Was the number more or less than you expected?

AD IMPACT

The debate about the impact of advertising is hotly contested, and not easily resolved. Let's look at the two sides.

ADVERTISERS SAY:

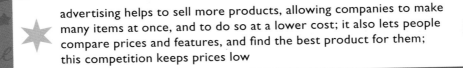 advertising helps to sell more products, allowing companies to make many items at once, and to do so at a lower cost; it also lets people compare prices and features, and find the best product for them; this competition keeps prices low

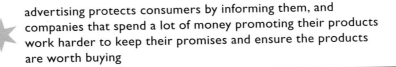 advertising protects consumers by informing them, and companies that spend a lot of money promoting their products work harder to keep their promises and ensure the products are worth buying

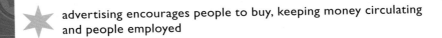 advertising encourages people to buy, keeping money circulating and people employed

advertising promotes products that can improve people's lives, and encourages people to strive for a better life

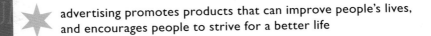 advertising allows people to consume media for "free"—including websites, magazines, TV shows, smartphone apps, and more; without advertising, consumers would have to pay the full cost for these products

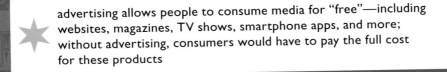 advertisers sponsor many sporting and cultural events (tennis tournaments, professional car races, concerts, film festivals); their support provides entertainment that wouldn't be possible if it relied only on ticket sales

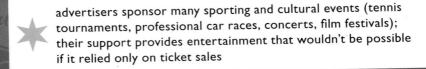 advertising can be used to promote important social messages (to encourage people to fight racism, or donate to charity, or exercise for good health), and it can be used as a public safety tool in emergency situations (recalling a faulty, dangerous product, for instance)

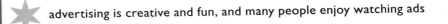 advertising is creative and fun, and many people enjoy watching ads

CRITICS SAY:

the money spent on advertising makes products more expensive; consumers are ultimately the ones who pay for advertising through higher product prices

advertising makes it easy for big companies (with lots of money to spend on promotion) to put small companies (which can't afford to advertise as much) out of business and limit competition

by encouraging people to buy things they don't need, advertising contributes to waste, creating pollution and damaging our environment; in the process, advertising can help push some people into spending money they don't have, which can have serious long-term consequences

advertising tends to show only certain kinds of people and to define beauty in a narrow way; it encourages people to be unhappy with themselves, to feel insecure and vulnerable, and it sometimes promotes stereotypes

to sell you more products, advertisers collect information on you, which may violate your privacy; the information may also be used in ways you don't want

advertising messages sometimes contradict the values of the events being sponsored (for example, drinking sugary beverages or eating fast food makes it harder to be a good athlete)

advertising encourages people to engage in activities that are unhealthy or dangerous (like eating junk food or driving too fast); the lifestyles promoted may not fit with such values as building caring relationships, or environmental responsibility

advertising is an annoyance and an unwelcome distraction

HEARTS OR MINDS

Those who defend advertising say people make rational decisions about what they're going to buy—that consumers consciously think about their choices and make decisions using their minds. Others argue that a lot of advertising is designed to engage people's hearts, not their minds. They suggest that ads affect us emotionally, not rationally, and convince us to buy products for the wrong reasons.

Can you think of an ad you saw recently that appealed to your rational side, giving you logical reasons to buy a product? How about an ad that showed an appealing image or situation, didn't tell you much about the product at all? Was one more memorable or persuasive than the other?

WHO KNEW? CLEVER CAMPAIGNS CREATE NEW NEEDS

Do you know how diamonds came to be the gem of choice for engagement rings? You might imagine that it's an old tradition handed down for generations. In fact, diamond engagement rings are an invention of advertising.

For centuries, opals, rubies, and sapphires were considered much more exotic than diamonds, and appeared more often in women's engagement rings. But in 1947, the big diamond producer De Beers began advertising the glittering white stones as the embodiment of love.

The company's slogan, "Diamonds are forever," cleverly equated the hardness and durability of diamonds with the notion of permanent love, and diamonds quickly became synonymous with engagement rings.

In advertising, a few well-chosen words, repeated many times, can have the power to change how people think and act.

If you really loved me, you'd have bought a diamond!

> Man, you're practically a walking billboard.

FITTING THE LABEL

Every time you put on a T-shirt or a pair of jeans showing a company's logo, you become a walking billboard, advertising the company's products. Check your closet to find out how much free publicity you're giving to brands. Think about the exchange: you get a T-shirt; the company gets the money you paid for the shirt plus the profile and exposure that comes from you wearing it. Your willingness to display the company's name on your clothes is the same as you personally endorsing the product and its makers.

DON'T TRY THIS AT HOME!

What do you think? Is advertising irritating and unnecessary, or enjoyable and useful? Maybe there's truth on both sides. Think about how advertising impacts your life:

1. Do the ads you see give you facts about products, or appeal more to your emotions?
2. What forms of advertising do you notice the most?
3. What kinds of advertising do you like?
4. If you hear or see things in an advertisement that you don't believe or agree with, how do you react?
5. Have you ever bought something solely as a result of seeing it advertised? Did the product live up to the advertising message?
6. Have you ever felt interrupted or annoyed by advertising? Why?

IN-GAME ADVERTISING

Movies and TV aren't the only places you can find advertising in the form of product placements. As early as the 1980s, the video game company Sega used banner ads for Marlboro cigarettes in its auto-racing arcade games. More recently, Barack Obama's 2008 and 2012 presidential campaigns placed ads on the boards of the football game *Madden NFL*. Advertisers also place their products and mascots within the games; in one boxing game for Xbox, players can unlock Burger King's mascot The King as a trainer, and in another popular game, the main character wears a T-shirt bearing the Axe Body Spray logo.

MOVIE PRODUCT WARS: THE MERCHANDISING MENACE

Once upon a time, movies were movies, toys were toys, and they had nothing to do with each other. Then *Star Wars* came along (the first movie came out way back in 1977), and things haven't been the same since.

George Lucas, creator of the *Star Wars* series, was the first person to turn the launch of a new movie into an advertising extravaganza. In addition to the millions of dollars spent making the film, Lucas spent additional millions promoting it. And not just through movie previews and TV ads. He also made special deals with all sorts of companies to produce *Star Wars* toys, clothes, and giveaway collectors' items.

This kind of advertising approach is called "cross-promotion," because it works two ways: people see a Harry Potter movie and are then more likely to want to buy wizard merchandise or the books; or they have always collected Pokémon cards, so they go to see the *Pokémon* movie when it comes out.

What does this add up to? The first *Star Wars* movie was one of the most popular of all time, earning millions of dollars and ensuring that the next five episodes would also attract a lot of viewers. But that was peanuts compared to the product sales. Together, the *Star Wars* movies have made $9 BILLION through the sale of character toys, posters, video games, laser swords, and a whole lot of other stuff. (For perspective, with that kind of money you could buy yourself and eleven friends each a brand-new $30,000 car every day for the rest of your life, assuming you lived another 70 years.)

Many other movies have followed in *Star Wars*' footsteps, from *Men in Black* to *The Hunger Games*. Nowadays, you don't even have to look up a movie to know what it's about: the advertising—in all its forms— will find you first.

BRAIN STAIN

Here's that quiz you might not have to study for: it tests your knowledge of famous advertising slogans. Cover up the right-hand column below and see how many of the slogans are familiar to you. Try testing your friends or family members, too. Lots of people say that advertising doesn't affect them. Next time you hear someone make that claim, test them to see how well they do on this quiz.

	SLOGAN	COMPANY/PRODUCT
1	Just do it	NIKE SHOES
2	Think different	APPLE
3	They're GRRRRRRRRREAT!	FROSTED FLAKES
4	I'm lovin' it	MCDONALD'S
5	Eat fresh	SUBWAY
6	Snap, crackle, pop	RICE KRISPIES
7	Bet you can't eat just one	LAY'S POTATO CHIPS
8	Easy, breezy, beautiful	COVER GIRL

CHAPTER 2

YOU'RE THE BULL'S-EYE

Once upon a time, advertisers didn't pay much attention to kids. They aimed all their sales pitches at adults.

But things have certainly changed. Starting in the 1950s, advertisers began to realize that kids not only had money of their own to spend, but they also influenced a lot of their parents' shopping decisions.

Imagine a dartboard with a picture of you and your friends in the center. You're now an important "target," and many advertisers think about your interests when designing their products and ads.

Research also tells advertisers that if they hook you when you're young, chances are better that you'll keep buying their products as you get older. This is called "brand loyalty."

Advertisers deliberately try to dream up ads that will help you convince your parents to buy things. They call this the "nag factor."

They also know kids can influence bigger buying decisions. Car manufacturers refer to 8- to 14-year-olds as "backseat customers" because they might cast deciding votes about which cars to buy.

WHAT ARE YOU WORTH TO ADVERTISERS?

Advertisers spend a great deal of money trying to convince kids to buy their products. But it's a drop in the ocean compared to the dollars they get back when you buy their clothes, candy, games, movies, technology, and food.

AMOUNT OF MONEY ADVERTISERS IN NORTH AMERICA SPEND TARGETING KIDS EVERY YEAR

$15 billion

$180 billion

AMOUNT KIDS IN NORTH AMERICA SPEND PER YEAR

YEARLY PURCHASING INFLUENCE OF KIDS IN NORTH AMERICA

$700 billion

CRADLE TO GRAVE

S_hopping experts_ have figured out that a customer who regularly buys from the same store, from childhood until she dies, is worth a lot. For example, if you spend $50 at the same grocery store every week, from age 20 to age 80, your lifetime value as a customer to that store is over $150,000. So advertisers try to come up with what they call "cradle-to-grave" marketing strategies that will help them turn you into a lifetime customer. And they mean "cradle" literally—even kids still in diapers and too young to walk or talk are considered marketing targets.

WHAT'S YOUR KEYWORD? HOW ADVERTISERS FIND THEIR MARKET

Advertisers have always looked for effective ways to reach the people who are most likely to buy their products. Today, they have many different options for how to do that.

In traditional media, like TV, advertisers have to make educated guesses about how to reach potential customers, based on what kinds of people like to watch certain shows. In turn, the money they pay helps to produce the shows, which are very expensive to make. The writers, directors, actors, and camera operators all have to be paid. The money that radio and TV stations get from soft drink, food, and clothing advertisers pays for salaries and buys equipment, sets, special effects, and much more. Only a few publicly owned stations—like PBS and National Public Radio in the US, or CBC Radio in Canada—rely on government or viewer funding for most of their programming. The others "sell" their audiences (that's you!) to advertisers.

I'll give you this if you give me him!

On the internet, there's much less guesswork involved. Advertisers don't have to use a particular website to find an audience. Instead, they focus on reaching people with very specific interests. How do they find these people? Easy: cookies—and we don't mean the chocolate chip kind!

Every time you visit a website, that website places a number of "cookies" (really, they're just files) onto your computer. Some of these are owned by the website and help your browser work—for example, they might remember your login name so you don't have to type it every time.

But others, called "third-party cookies," are owned by companies that keep track of which websites you visit. Many of these cookies transmit information to online ad networks, which place ads on a variety of sites. The cookies monitor all the things you do online: where you go, how long you visit, and what keywords you search. Then, the next time you look at a website featuring ads from the online ad network that owns your cookies, you'll see ads specifically tailored to what they believe will interest you.

So let's say you have a third-party cookie from Flashy Ad Network on your computer, and then you search for the latest Marvel comic book and visit an online retailer that sells comics. The next time you visit ANY website where Flashy Ad Network places ads, you'll see promotional messages from Flashy's clients who want to advertise to people who search for comic books.

But that doesn't mean you'll *just* see ads for comic books. You'll also see ads for companies who believe comic book fans will buy *their* products—maybe nacho chips, BMX bikes, and video game consoles. Why do advertisers think comic book fans will also like these things?

Because other people who searched for comic books also searched for chips, bikes, and PlayStations—and third-party cookies caught them doing it.

If you are a kid, your computer is being fed way more cookies than an adult's; one study found that websites catering to young people are the worst offenders, with one popular kids' site installing 248 tracking cookies on each visitor's computer!

Even if you block your computer from accepting third-party cookies (you can do this in the preferences section of most popular browsers), online advertisers can still target you in other ways. For example, if you search for something like "T-shirts" on Google, ads related to that word will appear alongside your search results. And if you've ever "liked" a fan page on Facebook, or filled out your interests, age, and gender, the social networking site uses that information to sell space to advertisers who want to reach people matching your profile.

Targeted ads aren't necessarily bad; no matter what, you'll be seeing promotions when you surf the net (unless you install an ad-blocking program on your browser), and sometimes it feels better to see ads for things you're interested in rather than ads for things you're not. But it's still important to know that you're a target, and the information you put on the internet gives advertisers better aim.

ADVERTISING TO ADVERTISERS

Your role as the product being sold to advertisers is really clear when you check out the kinds of ads that media companies themselves use to attract advertisers. A TV sports network promoting its airtime to potential advertisers promised: "We deliver the male." In other words, male sports fans are the product that the sports network is selling to advertisers. Facebook suggests that advertisers can "connect with more than 800 million potential customers" and "select" their audience "by location, age and interests."

~~DON'T~~ TRY THIS AT HOME!

If you want to experiment with how your online activities affect the ads you see, try changing your age on Facebook—pretend you're 57, or 82!—or search for things you normally wouldn't (say, broccoli, or classical music). Chances are you'll see some different ads alongside your newsfeed next time!

FAST FOOD

When you think about some of the techniques used by fast-food advertisers—bright colors, fun characters, movie tie-ins, and toys—it's pretty obvious they're trying to appeal to kids. On the web, fast-food chains target kids as young as age two with games and virtual worlds. With smartphone apps, companies can even send you a promotional text when you're walking by a restaurant. Much of this advertising is for junk food, like french fries and sugary cereal—exactly the kind of stuff doctors encourage us to avoid. Advertising's not entirely to blame for people eating too much junk food, of course. But you don't have to be Einstein to figure out that fast-food promotions have an impact.

Kids in North America see 10,000 food commercials and 1,500 fast-food commercials on TV each year

40% of children in the US aged 2–11 ask their parents to go to McDonald's at least once a week

In 2009, the fast-food industry spent $4.2 BILLION on marketing and advertising

1 IN 3 kids in North America are overweight or obese

Kids saw 34% more fast-food ads on TV in 2010 than in 2003

Number of kids in the US aged 2–11 who visit McDonald's websites every month: 365,000; kids aged 12–17: 294,000

FOR YOU, NOT THEM

Advertisers *think a lot* about exactly what they should say in their ads to persuade you to part with your allowance. For instance, they know that when adults disapprove of a certain kind of activity (such as staying up late, or substituting junk food for veggies), that might make it even more appealing to kids.

Advertisers know that kids are constantly being told what to do—by their parents, their teachers, their coaches. So many of them try to feature kids who are on their own, in control, and not having to answer to adults. They look for ways to make you feel they're your friend and ally, and that they feel the same way about things as you do.

But no matter how cool or fun ads appear to be, or how sympathetic they are to you and the things you care about, it's important to remember that what the advertisers care about most is your money.

IT'S EVERYWHERE!

It's getting harder and harder for advertisers to stand out, so they're getting more and more creative about where to place their ads. Sometimes, they display products in TV shows or movies.

Sometimes they'll place "pop-under" ads on websites, so that when you close your browser window, there's another window open with their ad.

Some put up ads in public washrooms, where you're pretty much a captive audience —there's nowhere else for you to look but at the ad.

ADVERTISING SCHOOL

Some people might think of school as a place where kids can focus on learning, free from commercial messages. But to some advertisers, when you're stuck in school—just like when you're in a washroom or movie theater—you're a valuable captive audience.

Many schools let advertisers promote their products on school property in exchange for financial support. Beverage companies, for instance, can give schools cash and vending machines. In return, the schools give the companies "exclusive rights," meaning that no competing drinks can be sold on school property. And a growing number of cash-strapped schools are selling advertising space in gyms, auditoriums, cafeterias, school buses, and even on lockers.

WHAT DO YOU THINK?

Should advertisers be allowed into schools? Does it make a difference to you if schools accept money for such things as computers, sports equipment, or music and art programs in exchange for putting company logos on team uniforms, wrapping textbooks in promotional messages, or naming food items in the cafeteria after characters in movies? Is it okay for schools to promise "exclusive rights," or is getting to choose between different products important to you? Or should schools be advertising-free zones?

(NOT-SO) GREAT MOMENTS IN SCHOOL ADVERTISING

1920s: Toothbrush companies invite themselves into classrooms, putting students through "toothpaste drills."

1998: A student in Evans, Georgia, is suspended for wearing a Pepsi T-shirt to his high school, which has an exclusive deal with Coca-Cola.

2013: Schools facing tough budget cuts might sell your locker to the highest bidder.

2060: Welcome to Cola High, the school of the future.

CHANNEL ONE

Is your school one of the more than 8,000 across the United States to subscribe to Channel One? This specialty TV service produces daily newscasts for middle- and high-school students on current issues, and gives schools free televisions and DVD players to watch them on. How can Channel One afford this? You guessed it—advertising. Teachers in Channel One schools have to make students watch the ads, stop them from channel surfing, and keep the volume turned up. Ever since the programs started in the early 1990s, Channel One's presence in schools has been a topic of hot debate. Here's how it shakes down:

CHANNEL ONE SAYS:	SOME EDUCATORS SAY:
TV is a good way to teach kids about current events because they're more interested in moving images than words on a page	the news items are too short to really teach kids anything, and the stories often don't have much to do with what students need to know
newscasts designed especially for kids are easy for them to understand and will help them to become interested in current events	research shows that kids' knowledge of current events didn't improve when they watched Ch. 1; 24 hours after the show, most kids couldn't recall the news items or their importance (but they did remember the ads!)
since schools are short of money, and advertisers are willing to contribute by helping to pay for much-needed equipment, everybody wins	schools are funded by the government, and paid for by everybody through taxes, so the time that kids spend watching Ch. 1 actually costs us all, because it's time during which they aren't learning useful things
teachers and students can use the equipment for other purposes, such as viewing other TV programs and videos	schools in poor neighborhoods, where students are already at a disadvantage, are even more likely to sign up with Ch. 1, meaning more poor students are exposed to the ads than other kids
since kids are exposed to advertising everywhere else, what difference does it make if they see it in school, too?	kids are already bombarded by commercial messages in the rest of their lives; schools should be advertising-free zones so kids can focus on learning

NOT ME!

Many of us deny that we're persuaded by advertising, but believe that it probably has an impact on others. Researchers call this the "third-person effect."

The fact is, sometimes advertising works and sometimes it doesn't. And not everyone is affected the same way, or by the same campaigns. What you like to do, how you feel about certain topics, where your family is from, and what kinds of things are important to you all influence whether a particular ad will make you want to buy a product or just throw a book at the TV.

But younger kids are especially likely to respond to commercials. And, not surprisingly, little kids who often watch TV are more likely to ask for and eat advertised snacks and cereals than kids who rarely watch. Kids are also targeted most online. (Remember what we said about those cookies?) In fact, more than 90 percent of pre-schoolers ask their parents for toys or food they see advertised.

Which makes sense. Because why would companies spend money on advertising if it didn't work? (In chapter 3 we'll find out more about how and why it does.)

PSSSST: PASS IT ON!

Advertisers who are trying to influence *young people like you know that "word-of-mouth" advertising is very persuasive. They've found from experience that if their product wins you over, you might tell others. Once you've seen their movie or bought their shoes, advertisers are counting on you to convince your friends to do so, too. In fact, this is one of the foundations of social media advertising: advertisers can create targeted ads that show you which of your friends "like" their product. They want *you* to do their advertising for them.

This approach doesn't always work, of course. Not all young people think alike. No doubt you and some of your friends disagree on your favorite music or video game, or wear competing brands of jeans. But you can probably find lots of things you do like in common. And advertisers benefit when you recommend your favorites to friends.

WHO KNOWS WHAT

Research psychologists believe that:

KIDS UNDER AGE 6

• may or may not understand that TV isn't real

• pay a lot of attention to commercials, which they trust

• often don't know the difference between ads and programs, noticing only that the ads are shorter

• often can't recognize marketing messages in online games and virtual worlds

KIDS AGES 6–9

• pay a lot of attention to commercials

• can tell the difference between ads and programs

• begin to recognize that the purpose of ads is to persuade

• sometimes don't recognize that online messages—or entire websites—are actually ads

KIDS AGES 10–14

• are less interested in commercials

• are very aware that the intention of ads, unlike programs, is to persuade

• can often identify and explain some persuasive techniques used in ads

• may actually be more vulnerable than younger kids to digital marketing that activates a subconscious emotional reaction

• often don't realize how their information will be used when they respond to advertising messages online or through mobile phones

MASCOT MANIA

Need more proof that advertisers believe kids are a valuable audience? Consider the number of companies that create toylike mascots to promote their products. Most of the time, these are designed with kids in mind. From the giggling Pillsbury Doughboy to Chester Cheetah and Tony the Tiger, an effective mascot can make an ad much more memorable.

These days, it's even more common for brands to associate themselves with popular cartoon and television characters kids already have a connection with. For example, McDonald's Happy Meals have featured Shrek, and Doritos packages have used images of the Green Lantern. And Sesame Street characters appear on everything from cereal to water bottles to iPad cases.

What's the payoff? One recent study showed that even though the products themselves hadn't changed, when a favorite character was stamped on a food item, kids thought it tasted better!

Whether or not the label or packaging boasts a mascot or a cartoon character, it's still the same thing inside. Companies just want you to think that their product is fun, or cool, or exciting, like the character.

GIRLS AND BOYS EACH SOLD SEPARATELY

Way back, the people who made TV shows believed that women and girls would watch anything that men and boys watched, but that if a show featured too many female characters and seemed designed for female viewers, no guys would be caught dead tuning in. This way of thinking had a big impact on the kinds of programs that got made. Early cartoons—like those featuring Bugs Bunny, Tom and Jerry, Mighty Mouse, and the Road Runner—had very few female characters.

And product mascots were almost always male. In recent years, attitudes have changed a bit: programmers have figured out that you can't predict what people will like just on the basis of whether they're guys or girls. Today's TV shows and movies feature more female characters, including some who kick as much butt as the guys! But toy and game commercials are a different story: many of them still make it look as if we come from completely different planets.

WORDS APART

When you look at the most common words used to advertise toys to girls and boys, the gender divide is hard to ignore.

Some of the top words in ads for "boy" toys include:

BATTLE
POWER
HEROES
ULTIMATE
ACTION

What's on the girls' list?

LOVE
FUN
MAGIC
BABIES
FRIENDSHIP
GLITTER

CHAPTER 3

AND NOW: A NEWER HAPPIER YOU!

Can you think of any recent or current ads that send the "Don't be a loser" message? Or how about ones that use the "Buy me and be cool" approach?

These strategies are just two of the many tricks and techniques that advertisers have in their toolkit. In this chapter we unpack that kit to examine the ways in which writers, directors, actors, photographers, food stylists, graphic designers, and special effects people "build" commercial messages. Who knows? You might discover a few pointers about the fine art of persuasion that you can use in your own life!

COMMUNICATION 101

Most of us communicate with other people every day, without even thinking about the process. But advertisers think a lot about how communication works. They're always trying to come up with new strategies to make sure their ads are effective. The smart ones conduct research. They survey consumers, asking them what commercials they remember, and whether they've bought certain products over the past month—and if so, why. For digital ads, advertisers track which ones get clicked on and which clicks lead to purchases.

Why do they go to all this trouble? Because the seemingly simple act of communicating is often pretty tricky. Just as messages can misfire when you're talking to your mom or texting with a friend, advertisers can make mistakes.

DID THIS AD WORK?

If you have a Facebook account and you've ever used a loyalty card at a store—the kind you swipe to get points or discounts—advertisers might be able to tell exactly which ads had an effect on you. How? Say you see an ad on Facebook for NO-BO Body Wash. You go to Shop-Mart and buy a bottle of NO-BO, swiping your Shop-Mart card to get a discount. Facebook can match information from your profile, like an email address or phone number, to the information Shop-Mart collects from your purchase. Then they can tell the makers of NO-BO how many people who saw their ad on Facebook went on to buy the product.

MESSAGE SENT   MESSAGE RECEIVED

BANNER BLINDNESS

Can you remember the last ad you saw online? Most people can't. In fact, studies have shown our brains don't consciously register advertisements on the web—our eyes tend to scan around them. This is so common that there's a term for it: banner blindness. We even tune out big, colorful, or flashing ads. So people who design online ads often try to disguise them, or make them harder to avoid. Ever been looking at a website and had a pop-up ad interrupt your reading, or cover up the link you wanted to click on? Shows you how hard web advertisers are working to get your attention.

Notice how there are two versions of the message to the left? The one sent, and the one received? That's because what you say or write may not be what the other person hears or sees.

"Noise" is anything that gets in the way of a message being received properly. Noise can be actual noise—like a lawn mower or siren drowning out what someone says. It can also be "emotional noise"— like when you're too worried about your lost dog to concentrate in school, or too excited about your team winning the game to hear what your brother is saying.

When it comes to advertising, noise can also be whatever distracts you from paying attention to the message. So if a fast-food restaurant runs a TV commercial aimed at kids, but the ad uses old-fashioned music, the kids watching might not pay attention. Or say an airline places a banner ad promoting travel to Europe on a website, and the site's main story is about a plane crash that killed 200 people. Readers may not even notice the ad because of the tragic story. And even if they do, they may not be keen to travel by air.

When good ads end up in the wrong places

CLIMB EVERY MOUNTAIN— UNTIL YOU GET A SALE!

Advertisers are keenly aware of the mountain of noise that prevents their messages from being received. In a sense, their job is to climb that mountain, to overcome the distractions that are constantly competing for our eyes, ears, and wallets. How do they do this? Check out the illustration to the right.

Once advertisers have us excited about the product, the top of the mountain is in sight. But the steepest part is still ahead: getting us to find the product, and buy it! Since ads can't actually pull you up off the sofa and drag you to the store, marketers concentrate on making it easy for you to access what they're selling. They make sure that their candy bars or magazines are available in many stores. Big companies often pay chain stores to place their goods at the ends of supermarket aisles, or at eye level, so it's easier for consumers to find them—and harder for smaller companies to compete.

Digital ads mean that advertisers can close the gap between sparking your desire for a product and letting you buy it. You can order from your computer or smartphone just by clicking on ads, and websites will often save your personal information and credit card details to make it as easy as possible for you to complete your purchase before having second thoughts. Some companies can send a coupon to your phone as you stroll by a restaurant or store, hoping you'll walk right in. New technology is constantly evolving to make it easier for advertisers to convince you to buy on the spot, while you're still in the "I want it!" stage.

THE STEP-BY-STEP JOURNEY UP ADVERTISING MOUNTAIN

STEP ONE: Attract our attention (it's a bit like finding the right hiking path through the woods).

STEP TWO: Engage our interest long enough to deliver their message.

STEP THREE: Convince us that the product really is as good as they claim.

STEP FOUR: Make us want the product or service they're promoting.

T-COMMERCE

Have you ever watched a TV show and thought you'd look great in the main character's jeans or cool sunglasses? Now, with just a few clicks, they can be yours. Several websites and apps let you browse clothes, home furnishings, and other products featured in TV shows and movies, and provide links to help you buy them. And soon you might be hearing more about "T-commerce," which lets you use your remote control (or smartphone) to buy things you see in commercials or programs directly from your TV set. Stay tuned for the latest developments...

DON'T I KNOW YOU FROM SOME . . . STEREOTYPE?

Advertisers don't have much time to relay their messages. Most TV commercials, for instance, are only 30 seconds long, and some are only half that. On the web, streaming ads often have a 10-second countdown until your video begins (and some even give you the option of skipping the ad, in case you lose patience and are tempted to click off the site). How can advertisers possibly tell stories—ones that are interesting enough to help them scale the mountain of noise—in so little time?

One of the strategies they rely on is the use of stereotypes. Advertisers understand that most of us will make predictable associations between certain aspects of a character's appearance and his or her behavior.

While stereotypes can be very convenient from the advertisers' point of view, they can also be destructive, reinforcing unfair and negative images about groups of people. Over the years, women have complained that commercials often portray them in limited roles—either as pretty objects to be looked at, or else as homemakers, in charge of cooking, cleaning, and

Know Your Advertising Stereotypes

nerd

clueless dad

hottie

grocery shopping. Similarly, men have complained about being shown as completely incapable of cooking a meal.

There was a time when it was rare to see non-white faces or people with disabilities in ads. That is changing as advertisers recognize the buying power of minority groups. McDonald's, for instance, features African-Americans, Hispanics, and Asians in many of its campaigns, and even relies on these customers to help design its messages. But many other advertisers still present minorities in less central roles. They often develop one campaign (featuring mostly white people) for the general market, and then create other versions (featuring African-Americans, Hispanics, or Asians) to target minority audiences.

Some ads also depict ethnic minorities in ways that reinforce existing prejudices. A study of video game promotions, for instance, found that black characters were often portrayed as violent and dangerous, while Asian characters were almost always shown doing martial arts. This is bad news— and not just for the people who are being stereotyped! Advertisers who insult potential customers—even if they do it by accident— aren't likely to be very successful at selling their product.

SOMETHING FOR EVERYONE!

ADAPT OR PERISH

You know the old story about dinosaurs—they became extinct in part because they weren't able to adapt to a rapidly changing environment. Over the years, advertisers have worked hard to make sure they don't repeat the dinosaurs' mistake!

Every time a new form of media has been introduced, advertisers have been quick to figure out the best way of using it to promote their products. When radio was invented, they created musical jingles to deliver slogans in a more memorable way. When TV came along, they added moving images and showed people benefiting from their products. More recently, advertisers have had to adapt to take advantage of constantly evolving digital technologies and trends. Sometimes, advertisers are even the ones driving new technologies that will let them deliver ads. But in other cases, they're struggling to keep up.

OLD MEDIA VERSUS NEW TECHNOLOGY

Over the last decade, major TV networks have sued satellite services and the makers of devices that allow viewers to skip over ads. Defenders of ad-skipping claim consumers have been avoiding or fast-forwarding ads since the remote control was invented, and they're just giving consumers what they want. The TV networks say that if their advertising revenue dries up, they won't be able to afford the huge cost of producing their programs. What do you think? Would you be happy to live in a world without TV commercials, even if it meant networks might not be able to produce good shows?

ADVERTISERS ADAPT TO THE WAY WE WATCH TV

When television was first invented, remote controls didn't exist. If you wanted to change the channel, you had to get up off the couch, walk to the TV, and switch the dial.

Remotes let viewers switch stations. Advertisers had to grab viewers' attention in the first few seconds of their commercials so they would want to watch.

Today, viewers with DVRs and certain satellite providers can skip ads entirely. In response, advertising has migrated from the commercial breaks into the programs themselves.

SHH, DON'T SPEAK

When the mute button was added to remotes, some TV advertisers created commercials that told the story of their product entirely in pictures. Nowadays, many ads convey their messages without dialogue—an example is Coca-Cola's long-running ad campaign featuring polar bears and penguins. As more and more companies sell their products all over the world, commercials that don't need to be translated from one language or culture to another are gaining in popularity. Translation is sometimes tricky; an image or slogan that may be seen as funny or clever in one place isn't always understood or appreciated in another. And in fact, some people who study how our brains respond to ads have suggested that ads featuring only pictures and music can trigger our emotions better than ads with words.

ON THE LANGUAGE LOOKOUT

On the other hand, language can be very persuasive. When commercials or other advertisements do use words, those words are very carefully chosen. Even a single word can make the difference between an advertising campaign that works and one that doesn't.

Words are especially important in web advertising, since most people are typing words into search engines to find what they want. Companies need to predict the most common words or phrases that people search for, and design their ads so that they will pop up alongside those searches.

Can you think of ads you've seen recently that included any of the following?

NEW
AMAZING
EASY
QUICK
NOW
GUARANTEED
LOVE
PROVEN
FREE
RESULTS
IMPORTANT

Research has shown that ads featuring these words are especially effective at attracting our attention and selling us products.

WORD WIZARDRY

Ever since the early days of advertising, when patent medicines were popular, some advertisers have used language to deceive people. They can do this in all sorts of ways.

BIG WORDS

Does your local convenience store label its slush drinks "Giant," "Jumbo," "Mega," or "Max" instead of "Large"? And have you ever noticed it's impossible to order a "small" drink at many coffee chains—the smallest size will be called "regular," "medium," or even "tall"? Does the use of one word instead of another make you feel like you're getting more?

In the last few years, some fast-food chains have cut back on using "large" synonyms in an effort to make their menu items seem healthier. In 2006, Wendy's stopped selling their "Biggie" french fries and soft drinks, which some people said promoted unhealthy eating and obesity. But Wendy's didn't actually change the size of the portions— they just renamed them with more neutral-sounding words.

Before   After

Which sounds better to you?

Recommended by 4 out of 5 Dentists!

Only 1 out of 5 Dentists hates this toothbrush!

MISLEADING STATEMENTS

The makers of a well-known headache remedy once claimed in a commercial that tests proved that no other pain remedy was stronger or more effective. In fact, the study had actually shown that all of the brands tested were equally effective. So while the ad didn't lie, it created the false impression that its pain reliever was better than the other brands.

CREATIVE MATH

Would you buy a snack that claimed to be "75% fat free"? Sounds like a good thing, doesn't it? What if the same bag had a label reading "25% full of fat"? Now it doesn't sound so healthy! And maybe a fruit drink claims it has "only 5 grams of sugar per serving," but unless you read the fine print on the nutrition label, you won't realize that their idea of a "serving size" wouldn't fill a thimble.

WEASEL WORDS

Words like "helps," "may," "often," and "part of" are considered vague. They're used to qualify advertising promises—to make them less definite. Phrases such as "helps with weight loss" or "may prevent tooth decay" sound good at first, but they certainly don't offer any guarantee. (You could just as easily say "may *not* fight tooth decay"!) Similarly, if the icing-covered pastry is promoted as "part of a nutritious breakfast," is it possible that the skim milk and fresh fruit you eat at the same meal are actually the nutritious parts?

GREENWASHING

Companies know that many people prefer to buy products that won't hurt the environment or expose them to harmful things. So marketers often use words that make their products seem environmentally friendly, even when they might not be. Would you feel better about buying a product labeled "natural," "clean," "green," "biodegradable," or "non-toxic"? In fact, some of the worst polluters, like oil and coal producers, airlines, and car companies, are some of the worst "greenwashers."

For instance, a bottled water company once ran an ad campaign with images of nature and the slogan "Every drop is green." What the company didn't mention was the huge environmental impact of its plastic bottles, or the fact that drinking water from a reusable glass bottle or the tap would be even better for the planet. And the makers of a certain brand of dish soap claim their product "helps save wildlife" because they have donated it to groups that clean up after oil spills. While the soap has helped get oil off many animals, the antibacterial varieties contain an ingredient called triclosan, which has been shown to harm animals and plants that live in water. Plus, the company that makes the dish soap has spent millions opposing environmental regulations.

SHOW ME THE MONEY!

Advertising is awfully expensive. Take TV commercials, for instance: in addition to paying for the same kinds of costs involved in making TV programs—the scriptwriter, director, camera operator, and actors, plus sound, wardrobe, and makeup people—advertisers also have to pay the TV stations for airtime. And the more popular the show, the more expensive the airtime.

DON'T TRY THIS AT HOME!

Often the biggest difference between products is in the cost—and usually, the ones that are advertised the most are more expensive! Next time you're in the supermarket, compare the ingredients on a can of no-name or store brand chicken noodle or tomato soup to the ingredients listed on a brand that you've seen advertised. What differences, if any, do you notice? If you put them—or competing cans of cola, or chocolate chip cookies—to a blind taste test, would you be able to identify which was which?

Next, make your way to the laundry section. Look for the small print on the detergent boxes that tells you the name of the company that manufactures each brand. You might be surprised to discover that one company makes both a nationally advertised product and a cheaper kind that you've never seen on TV. In fact, the products may be virtually identical. The cheaper one is designed to appeal to shoppers who are especially concerned about price, while the more expensive, advertised detergent is targeting consumers who may have more money to spend on perceived quality.

The annual Super Bowl football game is kind of like the Olympics for advertisers. They know a huge number of viewers are in front of their TV sets, and they use the opportunity to roll out new campaigns, often featuring celebrities or other attention-getting strategies. Some of the ads are so creative that there are people who watch the Super Bowl for the ads instead of the football! Getting a commercial in front of that many eyeballs costs a lot of money, but makes sense—and cents!—for advertisers.

But what does all this mean for consumers? After all, we're actually the ones who end up paying for advertising. When we buy a product, the price we pay includes the costs of promoting it. In fact, between 20 and 40 percent of a product's price is spent on its advertising. So if you pay $60 for a video game or a pair of jeans, as much as $25 of your money may actually be going toward the company's efforts at getting you to buy the product in the first place!

JEANS $60

FABRIC
LABOR
SHIPPING
RETAIL: $35
CONVINCING YOU TO BUY THESE: $25

BREAKING DOWN THE NUMBERS

SITCOMS

COST OF A 30-SECOND AD:

$500,000

AMOUNT A POPULAR SITCOM COSTS TO MAKE PER EPISODE:

$13 million

AMOUNT THE NETWORK EARNS FOR EVERY AIRING OF EACH EPISODE IF IT SELLS EIGHT 30-SECOND SPOTS:

$4 million

SUPER BOWL

COST OF A 30-SECOND AD:

$2 million

AVERAGE NUMBER OF VIEWERS FOR THE ANNUAL SUPER BOWL FOOTBALL GAME:

130 million

AMOUNT IT COSTS AN ADVERTISER TO REACH EACH SUPER BOWL VIEWER:

• ← 1.5 cents

WHAT ARE WE, COWS?!

Branding is a term that advertisers borrowed from the ranch. Its original meaning referred to the act of burning the rancher's identifying symbol into the flesh of a cow—leaving a permanent mark so everyone would recognize whose cow it was. Check out your shoes, computer, bike, and TV. Chances are, their brands are clearly displayed.

The ranchers' practice actually has more in common with advertising's version of branding than you might think. When companies create a product, or a line of products, part of their goal is to make the name and logo of their product so familiar to you that it's "burned" into your memory, permanently. Just as with the cow, they want you to recognize their brand forever.

Some companies have been amazingly successful at this. Nike's brand, for instance, is represented by its distinctive "swoosh." The symbol is so simple, and it's seen so often and in so many places, that most of us automatically associate it with the company's name and athletic wear. And not just in North America, but around the world.

In fact, some of the most effective logos have become a new kind of international language—the symbols are recognized by people from many different cultures who speak languages other than English. Advertisers are getting so good at "branding" their products that recent research has found that even babies as young as six months of age can recognize images of corporate logos and mascots.

BRAND ENGAGEMENT

Companies want you to form an emotional attachment to their brands, so that you trust them and identify with them. They encourage this through how they present and promote their products, and, increasingly, by engaging customers through social media. Do you always buy the same kind of jeans or sneakers, or prefer one brand of soft drink over another? Is that because you think the product is of better quality, or are you responding to something about the brand's image—its advertising, logo, or packaging? If your favorite maker of jeans started promoting a totally unrelated product—say, a fragrance—would you be likely to buy it?

COUNTING ON STAR POWER

When you hear the names "Beyoncé" or "Taylor Swift," do you think "pop star" or "salesperson"? Actually, they're both. And like many famous entertainers, these two singers may well make more money from their multimillion-dollar sales jobs (appearing in ads for Pepsi soft drinks, L'Oreal makeup, and CoverGirl cosmetics) than they do from making music.

Athletes are also popular among advertisers, and many companies have recruited high-profile sports stars to endorse their products. Hockey great Sidney Crosby has signed endorsement deals with companies including Reebok, Gatorade, and Tim Hortons. And basketball star Kobe Bryant has lent his name, face, and reputation to McDonald's, Adidas, Nike, Sprite, and even the video game *Guitar Hero*.

Many celebrities and sports stars go beyond endorsing a product to actually having their own product lines—such as clothes, shoes, and fragrances—which they often claim to design themselves. While it's possible some celebrities are talented at designing clothes as well as at singing or shooting hoops, many just lend their valuable names and images to products designed by someone else.

Does it make sense that more people would buy a product when encouraged to do so by someone famous? Does it pay off for companies who hire celebrities? Surveys have shown that about one in four people have bought a product because a celebrity endorsed it—and younger people are more likely to be persuaded by a celebrity they like.

But other research shows that not all celebrity endorsements are effective. People viewing the ads generally have to believe that the celebrity being featured truly uses the product, and knows a lot about it.

So a fashion model, for instance, might be effective at promoting a new clothing line, but not as convincing when encouraging people to buy hamburgers or french fries!

Also, people have to have a good opinion of the celebrity. It can be embarrassing for a company if the sports star endorsing their product gets caught using steroids, or if the movie star who designed their line of shoes does something stupid. Sometimes companies have dumped celebrity endorsers out of concern that bad behavior would damage their brand.

REPEAT AFTER ME

Research also shows that the more a person hears or reads about a product, the more appealing it becomes. A single advertisement is almost never effective on its own; repetition is key. For instance, by advertising steadily for six consecutive months, A&W Root Beer increased its share of the root beer market by 35 percent.

Frequency is important for online advertising, too. For one thing, advertisers need to repeat their message on different sites, since you might not be visiting the same ones every day. They also know that putting an ad online doesn't guarantee you'll see it. They invest in a lot of research to figure out the times of day or days of the week when you're most likely to notice and remember their ads, and then repeat their messages during those peak periods.

On the other hand, too much repetition can cause a campaign to become annoying. Have you ever gotten so fed up with hearing the same jingle over and over again that you switched the channel? Another problem with too much repetition is that an ad can become so familiar people stop noticing it altogether.

To avoid this problem, advertisers develop slightly different versions of the same ad, so the product name and slogan are repeated and remembered, but the variation will hopefully keep people paying attention.

TRICK OR TREAT?

Have you ever convinced your parents to buy you a game or toy you saw advertised on TV and then been really disappointed when you played with it at home? Either the game or toy didn't do what the ad suggested it would, or it just wasn't nearly as fun as it seemed when you watched the ad?

Advertisers employ all sorts of special audiovisual effects to make toys or games appear to be better or more fun than they actually are. Next time you're watching your favorite TV show, pay special attention to the commercials. If you turn off the sound during the video game ad, does it affect how exciting the game looks?

And check out the toy ads targeted to younger kids. Notice the kinds of camera angles used. Sometimes advertisers will make their products look bigger than they actually are by positioning the camera at an angle and shooting the toys from below.

Another common tactic is to show a toy—whether it's an action figure or a new fashion doll—surrounded by an elaborate set and all sorts of accessories that are sold separately. Even though the commercial might be promoting the main toy "for only $29.99!" you'd have to buy all of those items if you wanted to re-enact the activity shown in the commercial. And that would cost you much, much more.

Too Good To Eat

Have you ever seen a hamburger or pizza in a TV commercial or magazine ad that looked too good to be true? Well, it probably was!

Advertisers hire special "food stylists" to apply "makeup" to the food, to make it look better than it actually is. Take that juicy-looking burger, for example. Food stylists will smother the meat patty with Vaseline to make it shine, glue extra sesame seeds on the bun, and place pieces of cardboard or plastic wrap between the tomato and the bun to keep the whole thing looking bigger and fresher than it actually is. In other commercials, white glue is used instead of milk so cereal doesn't get soggy; chicken legs are injected with mashed potatoes so they look plumper; hot cocoa is made with dish-washing liquid so the bubbles last longer; and lipstick is applied to strawberries to make them redder.

Go figure: to make the food look more appetizing, they actually make it inedible.

Pucker up!

STRATEGY TOOLBOX

Advertisers have a lot of other strategies in their toolbox— no doubt you'll recognize some of them. What ads or commercials have you noticed lately that try to appeal to you in the following ways?

PRODUCT WARS

The "my dingle's better than your dingle" approach: this tactic can feature a product demonstration or a taste test to support the claim in the ad. The advertiser's hoping that the next time you're faced with a choice between one brand and the other, you'll remember the comparison from the commercial and buy the "better" product.

HEART TUGGERS

Even if there's no violin music, you'll recognize this kind of commercial by its personal story. Designed to put a lump in your throat, these ads (for such things as long-distance phone service or charity fund-raising) play on your feelings, hoping to create a positive emotional connection between you and the product or service.

EXCITEMENT PLUS!

This is the kind of ad that seems to be shouting, "Get down and party!" Lively music and lots of activity—often involving a fun atmosphere or great sports shots—are used to make you think that buying the product will guarantee you a really great time.

STATS UNLIMITED

Also known as "You're too smart to be fooled by advertising" ads. These messages flatter your intelligence by using experts and statistics to help you make a "rational" decision. "Nine out of ten dentists agree…" says the headline, or "Selected Car of the Year by automotive journals across the country…"

THE COOL FACTOR

Ah, yes, the tried-and-true "how not to be a geek" strategy. You've seen these ads: the awkward kid suddenly becomes hip by drinking the right soda, or wearing the right clothes.

FUNNY BONE

A humorous ad can attract your attention, and maybe even get you to talk it up or share it with friends. By making you laugh, an ad can convince you that the product itself is approachable and cool. But do you always remember the product, or just the funny joke?

THE NOSTALGIA EFFECT

As part of the marketing campaign for the movie Toy Story 3, Disney created fake commercials for toys from the 1980s, then uploaded them to YouTube through anonymous users. The ads were designed to appeal to people who remembered similar ads from when they were kids. The twist? They never once mentioned the new movie—but they went viral, and got people talking.

TURNING CATERPILLARS INTO BUTTERFLIES

From Cinderella to Spider-Man, people *love* stories that feature transformation. Advertisers have figured this out. That's why showing someone or something being changed in a dramatic way has become a common promotional strategy. You've seen the "before" and "after" photographs in magazines showing the effect of a new shampoo or skin cream. In the TV version, a problem is solved (chewing gum gets rid of bad breath) or a riddle is answered (the secret to the neighbor's weight loss is revealed).

The "solution" part of the ad usually implies not just shinier hair, whiter clothes, or a newer, faster car, but that we can receive other things that deep down most of us want even more: to fit in, to be loved and accepted, to be good at something, to have fun, to contribute the happiness of others, to be successful.

In fact, some people think that this aspect of advertising is what makes it so powerful. They point out that if people didn't care about these things, advertising wouldn't have so much influence over us. But because we DO care, we're vulnerable to messages promising that our lives could be richer and more exciting.

Of course, most of the time, ads don't come right out and make such promises in so many words. Instead, they paint a picture of good times and warm feelings. They encourage us to imagine ourselves in the situation we're watching, and to believe—without even realizing it—that we can experience the love and success we're witnessing by buying the products they are selling.

When we stop to think about it, of course we know it's not that easy. But we see so many ads that we rarely have time to stop and think about them critically.

DOES SEX REALLY SELL?

"Sex sells" is an advertising expression that's been around for a long time. It's used to explain the appearance of nearly naked models in ads selling everything from shampoo to wristwatches. The saying is based on the belief that exposed skin will attract people's attention.

In fact, although an image of a sexy model on a billboard will get noticed, it won't always help to sell the product. Studies show that people might remember the model (and the absence of clothes) but they often won't recall what was being promoted or why they should buy it. And some people find the use of sex in advertising offensive, especially if the product has nothing to do with sexuality. Their negative reaction makes them less likely to buy what's being sold.

MEASURING UP

You know from looking around you on the bus or at the local swimming pool that human bodies and faces come in all shapes and sizes. But in the world of advertising, the vast majority of people you see are exceptionally beautiful and extraordinarily thin.

Advertisers think that you'll be more likely to buy products from good-looking people than from average or unattractive people. And they may be right. The trouble is that the pictures of perfection—in movie posters and fashion ads, especially—can mess with your mind.

We've already heard how some advertisers deliberately set out to exploit your fears of being labeled a "loser." That's because they know that it's easier to sell everything from jeans and makeup to diet foods and plastic surgery to people who are afraid they're ugly or uncool.

But, in addition to being convinced to buy products that may or may not improve their appearance, some people are actually becoming ill in their quest to have a "perfect" body or face.

You've probably heard about eating disorders. They mostly affect girls and young women who start to see their bodies in a really distorted way, as if they're looking into a funhouse mirror that makes them seem fat, even if they're not at all. As a result, they adopt extreme dieting or exercise strategies. Guys are sometimes affected by this too, although they're more likely to become convinced that they're too skinny. This can lead them to take special food supplements and drugs that promise to build muscles. Unfortunately, the supplements and drugs can have very serious side effects.

Ads don't cause these problems all on their own; other factors are always involved. But lots of health-care experts agree that commercial messages play a role. Studies have even shown that people feel worse about themselves after they've looked at pictures of thin models in ads.

So here's something to keep in mind: when you look at a magazine or billboard ad of a beautiful model—male or female—chances are the image has been altered in a big way. First of all, the model has been professionally made up with loads of cosmetics and photographed under especially flattering lights. Probably the photo itself has been digitally enhanced. Such techniques are commonly used in advertising, even if few of us realize it—or consciously think of it every time we take in an ad. But there *are* companies that are trying to open people's eyes to the truth about beauty in advertising. As part of its "Campaign for Real Beauty" a few years ago, Dove soap created a one-minute video called "Evolution" that showed this transformation happening on fast forward. Still available online, it's a useful reminder of how unrealistic the images in beauty advertising really are.

PUFF-BUSTERS!

In 2004, Dove's "Campaign for Real Beauty" print and billboard ads featured non-models with a variety of body types and skin colors, posing in their underwear. The campaign was intended to counteract the unrealistic beauty ideals that encourage women and girls to feel insecure about their own appearance. The approach was so unusual that it helped to increase Dove's sales. Since then, some other companies have used fuller-figured models in their ads. Although many people criticized the campaign as nothing but a clever marketing strategy, it did prove that ads don't have to use thin models to get people's attention.

RESULTS NOT AS PICTURED

You might know from playing around with photo apps or image editing programs that it's easy to change the way someone looks in a photo. People who design ads have lots of tools to make photos look better. They can remove pimples, wrinkles, or shadows. They can also shave off pounds, change the shape of facial features, and make skin look lighter or darker. In recent years, some people have complained about images that are too "photoshopped," saying that they present a completely artificial standard of beauty. Photo trickery can also exaggerate the benefits of products—for example, images in mascara ads have been digitally altered to make eyelashes look longer. In response to consumer pressure, advertising regulators in some countries, including the US, have moved toward banning misleading photo editing.

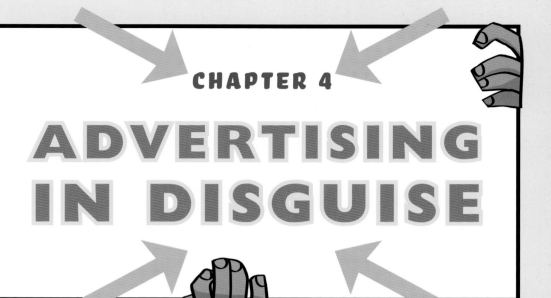

CHAPTER 4

ADVERTISING IN DISGUISE

What do advertisers have in common with spies? To be successful, both must master the art of deception. And some ad makers are sneakier than computer hackers when it comes to using strategies that will trip us up.

They know that the more conscious we are of the fact that they're trying to sell us something we may not need, the harder it will be to convince us to buy. They also recognize that we're increasingly wise to their methods, and know that the promises in their ads are designed to part us from our money. That's why advertisers are always on the lookout for new and unusual places to sneak in a promotional message, without making it obvious that they're doing so. They dress up their sales pitches in all sorts of "costumes" by giving them bit parts in movies and TV shows, making them look like games or news stories, disguising them as tweets or Facebook updates—or even paying the person next to you to rave about their products. It's like Halloween all year round!

GUERRILLA MARKETING

Some of these strategies are referred to as "guerrilla" (pronounced "gorilla," but having to do with rebel fighters, not apes!) marketing campaigns. A guerrilla campaign is any kind of unconventional way of getting an advertising message across. Advertisers know that we're so used to seeing ads in the usual places that we often tune them out. If they take us by surprise, the message is more likely to stick. Guerrilla marketing can range from street campaigns—like posters, graffiti, stickers, and handing out free products—to highly imaginative, interactive, and unique stunts. For instance, in 2009, to promote the Discovery Channel's "Shark Week" programming, an advertising agency created surfboards that looked as if they had been bitten by sharks

and scattered them around public beaches. And Colgate, which makes toothbrushes and toothpaste, once inserted popsicle sticks shaped like toothbrushes into ice cream bars; when people finished eating the ice cream, they saw the message "Don't forget Colgate." For a relatively low cost (compared to producing and airing TV ads, for instance), campaigns like this can generate a lot of attention and buzz for a product.

Some companies have used a combination of guerrilla marketing tactics and hidden cameras to capture the reactions of their unsuspecting audiences. Coca-Cola placed specially designed vending boxes, which they call "Happiness Machines," on several college campuses. Students who inserted change to buy a Coke were rewarded with two sodas for the price of one. Other vending machines had a person inside who would hand out food, flowers, and toys. Hidden cameras captured the students laughing and sharing the items with other students around them. These "real-life moments" were then aired in Coca-Cola commercials on TV and YouTube. By showing ordinary people reacting spontaneously to its brand, Coca-Cola created positive feelings toward its product.

Can you hold the mustard?

GUERRILLA GAFFES

Sometimes guerrilla campaigns can backfire. In 2007, the makers of a late-night cartoon show called *Aqua Teen Hunger Force* decided to try something new. Light-emitting signs featuring one of the show's characters were placed in various public spaces around 10 major American cities. In Boston, the signs were mistaken for bombs and detonators, forcing bomb crews and firefighters to shut down neighborhoods and close major subway stations to deal with the "situation."

GOING UNDERCOVER

In a sneakier form of guerrilla promotion—often called stealth marketing or buzz marketing—the people behind the message don't want you to know that you're being marketed to at all. Companies know that word of mouth is the most effective form of advertising: you're more likely to believe a recommendation from a friend or an ordinary person than from an ad. So marketing companies hire "ad spies" to use a product in public and engage people in conversations about it—usually without disclosing that they're being paid to promote it.

The stealth approach has received mixed reviews. Some consumer activists think the practice is dishonest and shouldn't be allowed. They argue that ad spies should have to tell people they work for the company. But the marketing firms that dream up these campaigns defend them, saying the actors aren't trying to sell the products, just demonstrate them.

What do you think? Would it bother you if you found out that the person you were talking to about a new bike or computer game was being paid to tell you it was great?

(NOT-SO) GREAT MOMENTS IN STEALTH ADVERTISING

In 2002, Sony hired 60 actors to pretend to be tourists and ask people to take their pictures with its new camera phone.

Marketers have hired actors to stand in lines and talk about products and sales, or hang around outside buildings eating new snack foods.

In 2006, young gamers posted "amateur" videos on YouTube about wanting PlayStation gaming consoles for Christmas. The whole thing was later revealed as an ad campaign.

Companies will sometimes pay other companies or individuals to post positive reviews of their products online, or even post reviews themselves under a different name.

VIRAL MARKETING

The goal of guerrilla campaigns is to "go viral": to get consumers to pass the advertiser's message along through their existing social networks, in real life or online. That way, advertisers don't have to do all the work of reaching people themselves, plus they benefit from the credibility of word-of-mouth recommendations. For example, companies might offer a special deal or let you enter a giveaway contest if you "Like" their brand on Facebook. The people in your network will then see your "Like" and might click on the page themselves. Or if you buy something online, you might get an offer for a discount or free sample if you "share" your purchase on a social media site like Twitter or Facebook. Say you got an email from a friend saying that they just bought a great product, and another email from a company about that same product. Which email do you think you would open, and which would you send to the trash? Whose opinion do you trust when it comes to deciding what to buy?

HAVE YOU BEEN IGNORING ME?

Website ads used to be confined to predictable places: along the top of the page (banner ads) or down the right side. But surfers' eyes got so good at avoiding those "ad zones" that now, ads are just as likely to appear in the middle of the page you're reading. On Facebook and Twitter, advertisers can buy "sponsored stories" or "promoted" tweets that show up right in your news feed or timeline. You're much more likely to look at such ads than the usual ones—and you might not even notice right away that they are ads.

ADVENTURES IN COOLHUNTING

Companies such as Reebok go into the hippest stores and clubs seeking out kids who are so cool they don't follow fashion trends, they create them.

Or they might go into online chat-rooms and pose as kids to gather information. They might even recruit kids to secretly collect information about their friends.

The companies find out what these kids are interested in. They get feedback about a new product they're starting to make and ask how it could be more "cool."

Then they go back to their factories and quickly begin manufacturing and advertising based on the advice they've gotten from the cool kids.

BRAND AMBASSADORS

Many fitness and clothing companies have "brand ambassadors": leaders in the brand's targeted community who are "hired" by the company to promote their goods for free. For example, a company that makes yoga gear might offer a local yoga instructor a discount on their clothing and equipment. People in her classes will see her clothing and yoga mat, and maybe ask where she got them. She's not getting paid, exactly, but she still becomes a walking (or bending!) advertisement to a targeted group of people who are interested in the same type of products.

PRODUCTS: THE MOVIE

Movies are also popular hiding places for sneaky advertisers. Have you ever seen *E.T.: The Extra-Terrestrial?* It's become one of the most popular movies of all time. It also represents a landmark case in the history of advertising.

The producers of *E.T.* approached the makers of M&M's chocolate candies and offered them an opportunity to have their candy featured in the movie. M&M's turned down the invitation. Instead, when the film opened on thousands of movie screens across North America and eventually around the world, a supporting role was given to Reese's Pieces candy. In a now-famous scene, the young boy in the movie leaves a trail of Reese's Pieces in his backyard in order to entice the lovable E.T. into his house.

As a result of the movie appearance and the "tie-in" advertising that promoted both the candy and the film, sales of Reese's Pieces soared by more than 60 percent.

HOBBIT-AIR?

In 2012, to promote the movie The Hobbit, Air New Zealand covered a Boeing 777 plane with an 830-square-meter (9,000-square-foot) Hobbit graphic and offered Hobbit-themed menus to passengers.

iPLUGS

In 2011 alone, Apple products (such as iPhones, iPads, and computers) made almost 900 appearances in TV shows and movies. In fact, they've been featured in one-third of all number-one films in the US in the past decade.

Movies haven't been the same since. "Product placements" can be found in almost every movie and television show you watch. They can be as simple as a Diet Pepsi bottle sitting on a person's desk in a scene, or a character referring to a particular store. But some movie franchises have taken product placement to a new level. The makers of the *Transformers* movies packed more than 70 brands into one 2011 film, including Apple, Hewlett-Packard, Porsche, eBay, *USA Today*, Panasonic, Burger King, Cadillac, Hummer, General Motors, Xbox 360, Mountain Dew, and Pepto-Bismol. Many critics and moviegoers objected to having to pay to watch what they said looked more like a two-hour commercial than a movie!

Actually, some movies may actually *be* two-hour commercials. Feature films have been developed about popular video games (*Resident Evil*, *Lara Croft: Tomb Raider*), toys (*Transformers* again, *G.I. Joe*), and even board games (*Battleship*). Are you watching a movie, or just a really long brand promotion?

As Seen on TV

Product placements are an increasingly important source of revenue for television shows now that many viewers are using DVRs and on-demand programming to skip traditional commercials. Sitcoms and dramas have featured everything from cereal and cars to hair spray and electronic equipment. And the products aren't just shown in the background—they often play a starring role in the plot. An entire episode of the sitcom *Modern Family* centered on one character's desire for an iPad, and another episode featured Oreo cookies prominently.

Reality shows, meanwhile, offer wall-to-wall opportunities for "brand integration" in everything from the products used in competitions to the cell phone services used to send in votes. A top reality

show can feature more than 500 instances of product placement in a season. Many reality shows have "main sponsors" whose names will be mentioned many times during each episode: *The X Factor* has Pepsi, for instance, *America's Next Top Model* has CoverGirl, and *The Biggest Loser* has Subway.

If TV programs are looking more like commercials, some commercials look like the programs, too. You might see ads that feature cast members from the show you're watching, or mimic the look of the program—so if you're fast-forwarding through the ads, you might stop, thinking the show is already on!

KEEPING GOOD COMPANY

Have you ever heard your parents complain about all the violence and bad behavior on TV? Advertisers would probably agree with them. And it's no wonder: studies have shown that ads are less effective when they appear during programs containing violence, sex, or drug use. So in 2010, Walmart and Procter & Gamble teamed up to produce a series of "family-friendly" made-for-TV movies that would feature characters using their branded products, including shampoo, cleaning supplies, and water filters.

The movies—emphasizing values like togetherness and honesty—were created to provide a "clean" environment for the companies' advertising and to build positive associations with their brands. So far, the strategy seems to be working; viewers of the first film, *Secrets of the Mountain*, were almost three times more likely to buy the featured products than people who didn't see the movie.

~~DON'T~~ TRY THIS AT HOME!

Next time you're watching a movie or TV show, keep an eye out for product placements, and count up how many you see. Compare the exposure a product gets in a TV show to the kind of profile it might be given in a commercial. Which one are you more likely to remember or talk about with friends? Do you have to hear a sales pitch in order to be persuaded? And does it make a difference to you whether it's a villain, a hero—or an alien!—using the product?

Sometimes product placement is done in a deliberately obvious, tongue-in-cheek way—as if to say, "We all know what's going on here, and we're in on the joke." For instance, in an episode of one TV sitcom, a character delivered a speech about the benefits of a certain cell phone service, then turned to the camera and, pretending to address the advertiser directly, said, "Can we have our money now?" The show was profiting from brand placement, and making fun of it at the same time. And the cell phone company looked like a good sport for letting itself be the butt of the joke. Does this kind of approach make you feel more positive toward the brand, or not?

MIND CONTROL AT THE MOVIES

In the 1950s, people got very excited about a thing called "subliminal advertising." James Vicary of New Jersey said he'd fixed up a movie projector with a special device that flashed the words "Eat popcorn" or "Drink Coke" onto the screen in the middle of the movie. The words supposedly appeared so quickly that viewers didn't notice them. This is where the term "subliminal" comes in; it means something that you're unaware of. Vicary claimed that as a result, soft drink sales increased by 18 percent at the theater and popcorn purchases shot up by 57 percent! You can imagine the reaction: advertisers couldn't wait to try it out, ordinary people became afraid that they were going to be brainwashed, and some governments immediately forbade theaters and television stations from using the technique. As it turned out, the whole thing was a big hoax.

Some people still claim to see "subliminal" words or images—often of a sexual nature—hidden in advertisements, but the visuals have never proven to be anything other than the product of overactive imaginations. The truth? Advertisers *do* use techniques to trigger our subconscious emotions, but the methods are far more sophisticated than hidden words or pictures. They're also far less subtle. If advertisers want you to think about a half-dressed woman when you look at their soft drink ad, they're not going to hide her outline in an ice cube—they'll put her front and center.

OLD SHOWS, NEW TRICKS

Advertisers sometimes "double-dip" product placements, digitally swapping one product for another. Digital product placement can be used to insert new products into previously aired programs or movies when they're shown in reruns, released overseas, or issued in a different format.

89

INFOMERCIALS

Have you ever come across a program on TV that looks like a talk show, a news report, or even a sitcom, but curiously, the entire show is devoted to talking about one product? You've probably encountered an infomercial ("information" + "commercial").

In the TV schedule, these shows are listed as "paid programs"— which makes it clear that they're actually ads. Just like normal programs, these shows will be interrupted by commercials. It's strange that a 30-minute commercial would have its own commercials, but one goal of the infomercial is to make you think you're watching a normal show—a show in which the people talking about a new beauty product or piece of fitness equipment aren't being paid to promote it!

Infomercials can be easily identified by the following signs:

in an amazing coincidence (not!), the commercials promote the same product as the show

as a dead giveaway, the show focuses on only one product

"how to order" information takes up as much screen time as the expert "interview"

they keep reminding you that supplies are limited so you'd better rush to the phone or website and buy the product today

Let's get real, ladies. Unsightly nose hair is a problem for ALL women.

ARE YOU TALKING TO ME?

Advertisers aren't allowed to target kids under the age of 12 with infomercials. In the United States, the Children's Television Act of 1990 made sure of that. Only 12 minutes of commercials are allowed during each TV hour designed to appeal to kids on weekdays, and only 10.5 minutes are permitted on weekends. For Canadian shows for kids, only 8 minutes of ads are permitted. There are other regulations, too: if children's television programs display an internet address, the site must be educational or related to the program; the programmers can't send viewers to a website that's intended mostly to sell or advertise products. Also, advertisers aren't allowed to use popular television characters to sell products in commercials.

CARTOON RULE BREAKERS?

Some people argue that clever advertisers are breaking the rules with program-length commercials for really young kids. They point out that kids' TV features all kinds of shows that were invented to help sell toys. *G.I. Joe, The Care Bears, My Little Pony,* and *Strawberry Shortcake* may look like regular cartoons, but they're actually produced by the companies who make the toys of the same name, as a sales strategy.

Companies have found other ways to reach kids before they've even outgrown their diapers. *The M&M's Brand Counting Book* and

The Oreo Cookie Counting Book are designed for toddlers who are just learning to count. In fact, when toddlers and parents read the books together, they need a supply of the sweet stuff on hand for counting—and, of course, for eating!

Some adults think these books are a great idea. "Anything that encourages children to be interested in reading is good," they say. But others—including many doctors—are dead set against them. They argue that it's not fair to target kids so young, or to encourage combining food with learning, which may lead to bad eating habits that adversely affect kids' health.

ADVERGAMES

Interactive games built around a product—called "advergames"—are another way for companies to target kids while getting around pesky TV advertising regulations. The earliest advergames, in the 1990s, were distributed on CDs inside cereal boxes! Today they can be found online on many websites aimed at kids, and as apps on mobile devices. They're often designed to promote fast food, sugary cereals, toys, and candy. And once they've got you hooked, they may prompt you to send electronic invites to your friends. While some kids probably enjoy advergames without even noticing their promotional messages, many learn to associate the brand or product with the fun and excitement of playing the games. And at some level, there's surely a link: one study showed that kids who played games based around Pop-Tarts and Oreos ate far more of those snacks than kids who played games featuring healthy fruits and vegetables.

SING-ALONG ADS

When you click on a music video online, chances are you're not thinking, "Hey, let's check out some advertising." But that's what music videos are: ads for songs. Music videos can be very expensive to make, and many are as creative and entertaining to watch as short movies. But recording companies give them to online video sites and TV stations for free. They know that every time someone watches a music video, it's like a three- or four-minute commercial for the performer.

And nowadays, music videos aren't just advertising music. Videos by top pop stars have incorporated product placements for such things as cell phones, makeup, and even dating sites. Lady Gaga's video for the song "Telephone," for instance, featured Miracle Whip, Polaroid, and Diet Coke. The money gained by featuring products gives musicians bigger budgets to make splashy videos, but some music fans have been turned off by the blatant commercialism.

IS IT AN ARTICLE OR AN AD?

Advertorials are the infomercials of the magazine world. They don't look like regular magazine ads, which usually feature large photos or other images with minimal text. Instead, advertorials look like regular magazine stories or interviews—lots of words with smaller images. They often give readers detailed information about a product or vacation destination, sometimes interviewing "experts." But once you start reading, you might pick up some clues that they're actually ads in disguise. Many magazines have guidelines saying that advertorials have to be identified as advertisements (usually in small print), and that they can't look exactly like the real stories in the magazine, but the differences can be subtle. Advertorials are everywhere on the internet too, as advertisers are crafting articles, posts, and videos with promotional messages, and paying popular websites and blogs to run them alongside their regular content.

The lines between ads and articles can get *really* blurry. Many magazines and websites feature what's called "advertiser-friendly" content: it isn't paid for or produced by advertisers, but it does showcase their products and present them in a positive light. It might be a roundup of new beauty products, for instance, or a gift guide for the holidays. Editors and writers for popular websites, blogs, and magazines are often sent free products in the hopes that they will write about them. And they like to publish this kind of material because it encourages companies to advertise with them.

Of course, instead of placing ads in regular magazines, companies can also create their own print or online magazines devoted entirely to their products. Some clothing retailers, airlines, and drugstores produce glossy "magazines" that include articles as well as ads. But if you read the articles carefully, you'll notice that they're mostly just ads with a lot more writing and fewer photographs.

That's weird—everyone in this magazine is wearing clothes from the same store.

IT'S ALL IN THE FAMILY…

Websites and magazines also provide "invisible advertising." For instance, many news sites and magazines are owned by larger companies that also own movie studios, television channels, and even toy manufacturers. Having all of these organizations in the same "family" makes it easier and less expensive for each one to promote its products.

How does it work? Check out the illustration to the right.

Even though the trailers shown on TV are the only obvious "commercials," the movie is being promoted in all sorts of other ways that don't really seem like advertising. And people who are exposed to even one or two of the interviews, articles, photos, or action figures, not knowing that all of the messages are coming from the same company, may get the impression that the movie must be a good one—just because everybody's talking about it.

FLAK ARTISTS AND SPINMEISTERS

You may have heard of the 19th-century circus promoter P. T. Barnum. Many people consider him the first master of "public relations," or PR for short. People who work in public relations help companies, organizations, and individuals present a positive image to the public. "Flak artists" and "spinmeisters" are slang terms used

THE FAMILY BUSINESS

"Dad's Studio" puts out a new movie called *Revenge of the Techno Wizards*.

"Mom Magazine" then puts a photo of the movie's director on its cover and tweets about the film's premiere.

"Brother's TV Station" airs trailers for the movie and broadcasts interviews with the movie's stars.

Finally, "Sister's Toy Company" creates a line of Techno Wizard character toys to sell to kids.

to describe them; they're said to "spin" good news stories about their clients and to take the "flak" when something goes wrong.

What's the difference between advertising and PR? Many people recognize advertising when they see it, but a lot of PR—especially if it's done well—isn't at all apparent to the average person.

A surprising amount of what we see or hear in information media—including news sites, newspapers, magazines, and TV and radio news and interview programs—shows up because someone has paid to get it there. They haven't produced a commercial or created a print advertisement, but they've persuaded the reporter or editor to profile their product or service as if it were genuine news. That story about a technology giant unveiling its latest gadget, say, or interview with an athlete whose clothes are covered in sponsor logos. Instead of spending hundreds of thousands of dollars on expensive TV commercials, they pay a fraction of that amount to a PR agency and get news coverage instead.

Thousands of companies, nonprofit organizations, governments, and individuals (ranging from politicians and business executives to actors and athletes) also use public relations campaigns to promote who they are or what they do through the news media. Strictly speaking, the campaigns aren't advertising, but in many respects they serve the same purpose.

NOW THAT'S A PR STUNT!

In 2012, the energy drink company Red Bull sponsored a man planning to skydive from the Earth's stratosphere. The free-fall jump set world records, and mentions of Red Bull soared on social media sites during and after the stunt.

WHO DECIDES?

Because *TV broadcasters,* websites, magazines, and news-papers rely heavily on advertising income, the companies who advertise regularly have a lot of influence—direct and indirect—over what gets aired or published. An advertiser who is spending a large sum of money to promote a product doesn't want the ad's effectiveness to be undermined by what comes before or after it.

For example, cosmetics companies have pulled their ads from magazines that didn't feature women wearing makeup on their covers. Liquor companies have threatened to withdraw their advertising from publications that printed news stories about alcoholism and the health problems caused by drinking too much.

You can see why this kind of censoring influence isn't a good thing for the public. We tend to believe that the news media are working for *us*—sharing information that's important for us to know. But their dependence on advertisers sometimes means that they put advertisers' interests ahead of readers' or viewers' interests. News about the side effects of a new drug or the performance of a particular car might get downplayed or left out altogether as a result of advertiser pressure.

CHAPTER 5
CAN THEY DO THAT?!

Have you ever seen a commercial that stopped you in your tracks and made you wonder, "Whoa! Are they allowed to put *that* on television?!"

Maybe you've done a double take at the sight of a billboard and thought, "That's how to make someone drive off the road!"

Or maybe you saw an online ad related to something you mentioned in an email, or searched for on another site. You might have asked yourself, "How do they know so much about me?"

If so, you're not alone. People have been upset by advertisers' messages, and their methods, for as long as advertising has existed.

Even though advertising has been around for thousands of years, rules about what advertisers could do or say were only introduced in the last century. The "magnificent promises" (or outrageous lies!) that Samuel Johnson complained about in the 1750s continued into the early 1900s. But by then some people were getting really angry about false advertising claims. They started to organize a protest movement and demanded that authorities do something to protect consumers from unscrupulous advertisers.

A BRIEF HISTORY OF ADVERTISING REGULATION

EARLY 1900s	As a result of public pressure, governments in the early part of the 20th century start to introduce some guidelines—especially regarding ads for food and drugs.
1910s–1920s	During and after the First World War, the rules are more or less forgotten. Some advertisers resort to scare tactics to try to stand out from their competitors. But people are used to hearing whoppers from the makers of patent medicines (remember chapter 1?), so it's hard to get them excited enough to lobby for change.
1930s–1950s	Because of the Great Depression, a lot of advertising disappears as people stop buying and companies go out of business. It's not until the late 1950s that someone first gathers the resources necessary to take an advertiser to court for making false claims.
1960s	Regulatory agencies are formed: Advertising Standards Canada and the Federal Trade Commission (FTC) in the US.
1970s	The US Federal Trade Commission finally starts making deceptive advertisers pay for their lies. The FTC also begins demanding that advertisers in certain industries submit evidence proving their ad claims.
2010s	Governments in the US and Canada propose various "Do Not Track" laws and regulations that would restrict how online advertisers can collect and share information on web users. Check the news for the latest updates...

LEGENDARY WHOPPERS IN ADVERTISING

In the 1920s, advertisers got away with some serious exaggeration. Scott Paper Company once told consumers that "a single contact with inferior toilet tissue may start the way for serious infection—and a long and painful illness."

Listerine went even further in the 1920s with an ad that told of a woman who came home from a party, caught a chill and died because she failed to gargle with the miraculous mouthwash!

In the 1970s, thanks to new regulations, the makers of Listerine were ordered to spend $10 million letting consumers know that "contrary to prior advertising, Listerine will not prevent colds or sore throats or lessen their severity."

THE DON'T LIST

These days there are all sorts of rules and regulations that advertisers are supposed to follow—especially when they're advertising to children. Here's what the rules say about how North American advertisers should behave when they're encouraging young kids to buy their products. (Canadian and US regulations are similar, but not identical. To find out exactly what's allowed in your country, check out the notes at the end of the book.)

Next time you're on a website or watching an online video or TV program designed especially for kids, pay attention to the ads. See if you notice the advertisers obeying—or disobeying—the rules.

1 NO exaggeration allowed. This covers not just what the ad says, but what it shows; for instance, the advertiser can't use special effects to make the toy look bigger, go faster, or do things—like come to life—that it can't really do.

2 NO promoting products to young kids if they are only suitable for older kids or adults.

3 NO telling kids that they "have" to buy the product, or that they "should get their parents" to buy it for them. An advertiser can say, "This doll is available at ABC Store," but not, "Ask your mom for this doll."

4 NO telling kids that if their parents don't buy it, they're mean, or if they do, they're more generous than those who don't.

5 NO featuring violence or other activity that's inappropriate for kids to see and that might frighten or confuse them.

6 NO promoting craft and building toys that are too difficult for most kids to put together. If the product does need to be assembled, the ad must say so using words that can be understood by the targeted age group.

7 NO using well-known kids' entertainers, cartoon characters, or puppets to endorse or demonstrate a product unless the character was actually created by the company specifically for the product—like "Mario" for the *Super Mario Brothers* video game.

8 NO showing stuff in the ad that's not included with the toy, unless it's clearly stated—such as "batteries not included," or "PlayStation sold separately."

9 NO showing dangerous activity. When ads feature cycling or roller-blading, for instance, the kids must be wearing protective helmets and/or safety pads. If they're jumping on a trampoline, adults must be shown supervising.

10 NO telling kids that if they don't buy the product, they won't be popular, or if they do buy the product, they'll be smarter, stronger, skinnier, or cooler.

11 NO using social stereotypes in ads or encouraging kids to feel prejudiced against a certain group or "kind" of person. Advertisers are also supposed to try to include kids of all colors and abilities.

12 NO using words like "rush down" or "buy now" to make kids think they have to buy a product right away. And no using words to make the price sound low, like "bargain price" or "only $2."

13 NO telling kids to call a toll-free line, give out personal information, or buy something off the internet without first telling them to check with their parents.

14 NO creating false expectations about kids' chances of winning giveaway prizes. Advertisers have to clearly state what the likelihood of winning a prize is.

15 NO using the words "new" or "introducing" for more than one year and no trying to convince kids that last year's toy is no longer any good now that a new model is available.

16 NO tracking kids' online activities.

JUST SAY "NON"

In many countries—Greece, Norway, Denmark, Sweden, and Belgium, for instance—advertisers are not allowed to target their sales pitches to kids at all! Even in North America, the Canadian province of Quebec forbids advertising to kids under the age of 13. Can you imagine what it would have been like to grow up without seeing commercials during your favorite shows? Would you have missed them?

Enter To WIN!*

* You are more likely to have this airplane fall on your head than to win this contest.

WHAT DO YOU MEAN, THERE ARE NO AD POLICE?

In the US, advertisers operate on an honor system; they're just expected to know and obey the regulations set out by the Children's Advertising Review Unit (CARU) of the Council of Better Business Bureaus, an industry organization. In Canada, every advertisement targeted to kids—whether television, radio, or magazine—has to be submitted to another industry organization, Advertising Standards Canada (ASC), for approval before it can be broadcasted or published. The advertisers even have to pay a fee to have their ads approved.

In both countries, there are also guidelines for how advertisers should behave when pitching their products to adults. Would it surprise you to learn not every advertiser pays attention to the guidelines?

When companies do break the rules, there aren't exactly any "ad police" patrolling the airwaves and the web, searching newspapers and magazines, looking through emails and text messages, or investigating billboards to give the offenders a ticket or lock them up. Most of the time, unless consumers (that would be people like you and me!) make a fuss, advertisers can just go on breaking the rules.

SO if we want advertisers who are stretching the truth or showing dangerous behavior to clean up their acts, we have to:

1 know the rules in the first place;

2 remember exactly when and where we saw the deceptive ad, and what it claimed;

3 know who to complain to;

4 take the time to complain;

5 do it in writing; and

6 if possible, share the complaint online or in another public forum, because advertisers are more likely to respond if they know lots of people are paying attention.

That's a lot of work for consumers to do. Most people who see advertising that they think is irresponsible or deceptive don't bother to tell the advertiser or the authorities. Instead, they just gripe to their friends. Or maybe they'll go a step further and write a Facebook post, blog, or tweet, which doesn't take much more effort and widens the circle of people who will hear their complaint. But still, those sorts of comments are bad news for the advertiser, because we're often more influenced by what our friends say than we are by advertising!

A NEW FRONTIER

Would you be surprised to know that advertising on the internet has to follow exactly the same rules as print, TV, radio, and billboard ads? Online ads aren't beyond reach of the law, and just like ads in any other medium, they can't be misleading or unfair, or make claims that can't be backed up. But on the internet, it can be more difficult to make individuals and companies stick to the rules. Because information and images cross international boundaries, it's not always clear how to enforce regulations established by any one country.

Of course, some kinds of online advertising are very different from TV or print ads, and the rules have had to evolve along with technology. For instance, have you ever spent ages searching for the little "X" symbol to close an annoying pop-up ad? There are regulations in the US that say online ads can't require a lot of effort or special knowledge to close. Ads that change your computer's browser or security settings are also not allowed.

ARE YOU BEING FOLLOWED?

But the biggest debate about advertising on the internet has to do with something called "behavioral advertising," and its implications for the privacy of web users. Behavioral advertising is when web companies and advertisers track information about what you do online on different sites, over a period of time, so they can figure out your interests and deliver ads targeted directly to you. Remember those cookies from chapter 2? This is where they play a role—along with their even trickier cousins, like "flash cookies" (which are harder to find and delete than regular cookies), "super cookies" (which can store information permanently on your browser), and "web bugs" (invisible files that record when you are reading a web page or email, and from what computer).

The biggest internet companies, like Google, Facebook, Microsoft, Apple, and Amazon, can put together a wide assortment of data about you. For instance, Google's range of services includes its search engine, Gmail (for email), Google+ (for social networking), Picasa (for photo sharing), and YouTube (for videos), just to name a few. If you use these services, Google can collect information from your emails, chats, videos, calendar appointments, friends and networks, search queries, location information, and much more, to create a detailed picture of you. This kind of information is very valuable to advertisers, and can be sold to them at a premium.

Why does all this matter? Maybe you think, "I have nothing to hide, so what's the big deal if companies are collecting information about me?" The problem is that we don't know what the information might be used for, who it might be shared with, or how long it will be kept. We don't even have a way to find out if the information companies are collecting about us is correct. Some people concerned about internet privacy say it's possible that something you inadvertently reveal through your online activities (maybe about your health, spending habits, or political opinions) could come back to haunt you in 5, 10, or even 20 years, when you're applying for college, looking for a job, applying for a credit card, or buying a house.

Many people are also concerned about the tracking of children who use the internet. Young children may not understand complicated agreements and disclaimers on websites, and some adults argue that children can't meaningfully consent to web companies gathering information about them.

Because of concerns about the privacy of citizens, there is a lot of discussion these days about regulating how advertisers can track people online. Canadian guidelines introduced in 2011 say that advertisers should let people know when they're being tracked, give them a way to easily opt out, and not track on websites aimed at children. In the US, rules have been proposed to strengthen privacy protection online, especially for children. As well, most web browsers now allow you to change your settings to disallow tracking. But not surprisingly, online advertisers and web and media companies have objected. They say the regulations would hurt their businesses and limit the many free services people can access online—including email, social networks, maps, and videos—which are supported by advertising. They also argue that they're trying to serve web users better by showing ads for things that will interest them. Stay tuned for updates—this fight probably won't be over anytime soon.

YOU ARE WHAT YOU BUY?

Companies can get a pretty good picture of us from our activities and purchases online, but so far they haven't been able to put together our online profiles with what we do in the real world. However, major credit card companies are looking into ways to combine the information they discover about you online with your credit card purchases offline, to come up with an even more focused picture of who you are and how they can advertise to you.

SOCIAL ADVERTISING

If you have a profile on a social media site, you might not know that just by signing up, you're agreeing to let the site collect information about everything you post or do, and use that information to create an anonymous profile that they share with the companies that advertise with them. You can usually find the site's terms and policies on data use by looking for a link in small print at the bottom of the web page.

And advertisers on these sites don't just advertise to you; they use you to advertise to your friends. With your approval, your friends can see an ad bearing your photo and name endorsing a product. If you really liked a product, would you be happy to broadcast an ad (starring you!) to everyone in your network? Or would you feel uncomfortable being used as an unpaid product spokesperson in ads tailored to your friends and family?

YOUR PAL SAM IS GOING TO THE G-MEN MOVIE—ARE YOU?
YES
PROBABLY

SPAM! WONDERFUL SPAM!

Click here for your free trial of canned mystery meat. Ever get emails like this one in your inbox? Or maybe sent to your phone by text? Spam is any kind of unwanted electronic communication, including ads and email scams. (Yes, it's named after the lunch meat, by way of a famous TV sketch from the British comedy group Monty Python about a restaurant that serves nothing but Spam.)

Spam accounts for a huge amount of online traffic: between 85 and 95 percent of *all emails* are spam! Most are filtered directly into junk mail folders or ignored completely. But spammers are counting on just a few people being interested in their products. Let's say that spammers send the same email to 10 million email addresses. If only 0.01 percent of those people bite, that's still 1,000 consumers, and all they had to do was press send!

For years now, internet service providers, security firms, and antivirus companies have been fighting against spammers, creating complicated blocks to identify spam before it even gets to your inbox, but spammers keep coming up with new tricks to get around those blocks. They might pretend the messages are from a celebrity, someone you know, or a company you've bought things from, to trick you into clicking on a link. Or they might use misspelled words to get around spam filters. It's a never-ending race between spammers and anti-spammers.

There are things you can do to reduce your spam intake. Protect your email address by not sharing it with people or sites you don't know, and by not using it on mailing lists, social media sites, or public message boards. Check your email account to make sure that your settings are high enough to catch spam, and read through the privacy policies of websites that ask for your personal information to make sure they aren't selling your email address to other companies. Above all, don't open any emails or links sent through spam, or reply to any of those emails! Even though most spam is harmless, some can put a virus onto your computer, or take your personal information and use it elsewhere in what is called "identity theft." Replying includes clicking on the "unsubscribe" button, because this lets spammers know that your email is valid and active, and you could end up getting even more ads for canned mystery meat!

CAUTION: FOUR-YEAR-OLDS ARE WATCHING

On the internet, at least you have a choice about which sites you visit, so you have some control over the advertising you see. You also decide which radio stations or TV programs you tune into, which comics, magazines, or newspapers you read, and which apps and games you want to use. But outdoor advertising—on billboards, transit shelters, or the sides of buses—is different because it's seen by almost everybody. You don't choose it, it's just there.

Due to this general exposure, some people believe there ought to be different rules for outdoor ads—especially because young children see them. They argue that sexually suggestive ads, or ones that show violent imagery or promote alcohol—all of which certainly wouldn't be allowed to run during TV programs or on websites aimed at kids—shouldn't be out in the open where kids can see them, either. What do you think?

Smart advertisers and billboard companies tend to be careful about what images they put up outside because they don't want to have to take them down if people complain. On the other hand, some advertisers have been accused of running deliberately contro-versial billboard campaigns just to attract attention and generate news coverage. For example, the animal rights organization PETA and the clothing company American Apparel have both been forced to take down controversial billboard ads after people complained.

In one Thanksgiving PETA campaign, billboards were placed around schools reading, "Kids: If you wouldn't eat your dog, why eat a turkey?" American Apparel, meanwhile, drew fire for billboards featuring images of young-looking women wearing little clothing. Even though the companies were required to remove their ads, they got as much or more attention because of them—through news coverage—than if they'd used less offensive images that stayed up longer.

What do you think of this strategy? Should advertisers have the right to put up potentially offensive ads, or should they be required to have their billboards pre-screened?

ADS IN STRANGE PLACES

Sometimes people are less concerned about what advertisements say than where they are. Can you guess which of the following promotional strategies generated the most negative reaction?

Pepsi and Coke ads painted on the Himalayan mountain range in India

painting an entire street—the pavement, the houses, the trees!—in Salford, England, the color of pink bubble gum in celebration of "Barbie Pink Month"

advertisements for a Batman movie projected on sidewalks

Although all three promotions got people upset, India's Supreme Court ruled that the actions of the soft drink companies had put the sensitive ecosystem of the Himalayas at risk. The court fined the makers of Pepsi and Coke for causing environmental damage.

WITH FRIENDS LIKE JOE, WHO NEEDS ENEMIES?

Perhaps the most abusive advertisements of all were the campaigns designed to get people—and especially kids— to smoke. It's not like we haven't all heard about the number of people who will die of smoking-related causes!

Not surprisingly, tobacco companies aren't allowed to advertise to kids—or even teenagers. In Canada, tobacco marketing is highly restricted, and only allowed in a few places, like bars, direct mail, and magazines and newspapers aimed at adults.

It looked cool when Joe was doing it!

Since 2010, tobacco advertising in the US has been very restricted as well. In Canada and the US, as well as in Europe, tobacco companies can't even sponsor sporting and cultural events.

Before these rules were developed, tobacco manufacturers tried a variety of strategies to attract the attention of young people. As one company marketing report stated, "Today's teenager is tomorrow's potential regular customer."

One tobacco company in particular developed a campaign designed to appeal to very young children. In 1987, R. J. Reynolds created a cartoon camel named "Joe" to promote Camel cigarettes. Joe was featured in a series of advertisements doing cool stuff, like playing in a rock band, shooting pool, and riding a motorbike. In addition to appearing in magazines and on billboards, Joe also showed up on T-shirts and baseball caps. In fact, the campaign was so successful that a study done only four years after the cartoon camel was introduced found that he was as recognizable to kids as Mickey Mouse!

Another study found that before the creation of Joe, less than one percent of smokers under the age of 18 smoked the Camel brand. Four years after the cartoon character was introduced in millions of dollars' worth of ads, more than 32 percent of the same group smoked Camel cigarettes.

There's no doubt that R. J. Reynolds was working hard to get kids to identify with Joe Camel so that eventually they would get hooked on Camel cigarettes. Fortunately, after many people complained, the US government finally told the tobacco company in 1997 that it had to stop using the cartoon character.

SMOKING HOLLYWOOD

When TV advertising of cigarettes was banned in the 1970s, tobacco companies turned to movies instead. Since 1989, cigarette brands haven't been allowed to use product placement in movies. And yet the smoking rate among major characters in movies is about 300 percent higher than it is among real people. Although cigarette smoking in North America is actually declining, over 80 percent of the top-grossing movies produced in the last decade have incidents of smoking in them! Which just goes to show that "reel" life is not exactly real life.

What's the big deal about smoking on the big screen? Well, studies have shown that the more incidents of smoking young people see in the movies, the more likely they are to start smoking themselves. In the United States, *every day* 3,800 young people smoke a cigarette for the first time. Because of this, some anti-smoking groups and researchers have argued that all movies with smoking scenes should be classified with an R rating. And starting in 2005, three major film companies—Disney, Time Warner, and Comcast—pledged to reduce the use of tobacco in their films. Still, in 2011, the movies from those studios had just as many incidents of smoking as movies made by studios without tobacco-reduction policies.

IF YOU CAN'T BEAT 'EM, JOIN 'EM

or years, health authorities have tried to come up with persuasive anti-smoking advertising campaigns. There are even laws forcing tobacco companies to cover three-quarters of their packaging with health warnings and images depicting the potentially devastating effects of smoking cigarettes. Some anti-smoking ads can be extremely graphic and in-your-face. What do you think? Are testimonials from real people suffering from cancer or other health effects more persuasive than talking with teachers or parents? Why or why not?

CHAPTER 6
YOU POWER

Sometimes—*maybe even often!*—an ad really gets on your nerves. Maybe you think it's misleading or irresponsible. Perhaps it shows certain people in a stereotypical way, or you don't like the values it promotes. Or maybe it's not the message of the ad that bugs you so much as where it appeared, who it's aimed at, or how often you have to see or hear it.

So what's the best way to get advertisers to smarten up? Getting in touch to let them know what you really like or don't like.

Back in chapter 2 we talked about how important young people are to advertisers—how they're always on the lookout for new ways to reach you and sell you stuff. The good news about this fact is that it means they care what you think. If you take the time to give them feedback, chances are they'll listen.

You have power. Let's call that power the "Three C's": Consumer Power, Companion Power, and Complaint Power. You're in charge of how and when they get used.

CONSUMER POWER

Every time you pull a quarter or a dollar or ten dollars out of your pocket, you're using your consumer power. You're deciding how and where and on what to spend your money.

But what then? What if you buy a game that falls apart after two weeks even though you used it exactly like the kid in the TV commercial did? Do you shove it to the back of your closet and then forget about it? Do you take it back to the store and request a refund? Or do you make a mental note of the name of the company that made it, and remind yourself to avoid wasting your money on their games in the future?

This last option is called a "boycott"—it refers to the decision people make to refuse to do business with a particular organization. In the past, people have boycotted TV stations for broadcasting too much violence; they've boycotted food and clothing companies for taking advantage of poor people in less fortunate countries; and they've boycotted perfume and beer advertisers for producing ads that portrayed women as if they were objects to be bought and sold.

Does it make much of a difference to a company if you stop buying their products or watching their shows? Maybe not, if you're the only one. But it's still worthwhile. Your choice to boycott gives you a way to say, "I think this company is irresponsible and dishonest. I don't support what they're doing or saying, and I'm going to do something— however small—to protest."

On the other hand, if you want your protest to make an even bigger difference—to change the way a company makes its toys or advertises its products—Companion Power and Complaint Power are good ways to increase your impact.

COMPANION POWER

Say you're at a hockey or basketball game, and you stand up with your arms raised over your head. The only people likely to notice are the folks sitting next to you or behind you. But if a whole bunch of people stand up all together or do a wave, everybody notices!

The same principle applies when it comes to consumer protest. Your broad circle of friends and acquaintances, your "companions," can make a difference. If you stop buying a product or tuning in to a TV show as a form of protest, your act won't attract much notice. But when hundreds or thousands of people make the same choice, companies pay attention. Advertisers have often responded to mass protests by changing or canceling unpopular ad campaigns.

SPREADING THE WORD

If you see an ad that makes *Ramma Gamma X Star* look like the greatest game ever, but you know that it's nothing like the ad suggests, you're likely to tell all your friends.

Then, if your friends tell other friends and their brothers and sisters, who tell their own friends, who then tell even more people...

Well, you get the picture—it's like doing the wave at the sports event—it's pretty hard to ignore!

A "wave" of consumer power—in which a lot of people stop buying a company's products—is more likely to get noticed.

COMPLAINT POWER

If you really want a company to change what it's doing— in an ad, at its manufacturing plant, or in another country—the best thing to do is to get in touch with the company directly. It's always best to put your complaint in writing. Most companies will have contact email addresses on their websites, or sometimes online forms you can fill out. And if more than one person writes to a company expressing concern about the same thing—combining Companion Power and Complaint Power—that's even better!

Social media sites, blogs, and online comments have given ordinary people a lot more power to influence companies' behavior. A post or tweet about a company's offensive ad or unethical practices can quickly go viral and create a public relations nightmare. Companies often have people on staff who search the web for mentions of their name and respond to complaints to try to keep bad buzz from spreading. If you have something you want to say, you can post comments about ads on your own personal page, which will reach everyone in your network, including people you might not see regularly. Or you can post comments directly on a company's social media page, send a tweet directed to them, or post on a website dedicated to product reviews. Then your voice could be heard by countless consumers around the world!

Let advertisers know when they're doing something right, too. If you see an ad you think is different and sends a positive message, tell the company so they know you support what they're doing. If companies know that people like seeing ads with non-stereotypical characters or positive representations of diversity, for instance, they're more likely to continue making those types of ads.

CAN YOU IMAGINE HOW POWERFUL THOSE PEOPLE FELT?

Often people are surprised to learn that a company will cancel an ad in response to just a few complaints from a handful of people. However, advertisers recognize that for every person who writes an email or picks up the phone to complain, there are probably hundreds more who are also offended. Smart advertisers often decide to pull the ad that caused concern right away rather than risk angering other potential customers.

HOW TO MAKE YOUR COMPLAINT COUNT

If you do decide to post publicly on a website or social media page, make sure that you get all the facts right, and that your comment is clear and well written. People won't take your complaint seriously if it's full of spelling mistakes or written in ALL CAPS. If writing's not your thing, you could make a video sharing your thoughts and post it somewhere people will see it.

Keep in mind that sometimes false rumors about ads or companies can get passed around, which can unfairly damage companies' reputations. If you see somebody else's comment on an ad or company and feel tempted to pass it on, do a little research first to make sure what they claim is true.

GETTING COMPANIES TO LISTEN UP

Some complainers are more effective than others. You may have noticed this in life generally: two people can have exactly the same problem with the way something is being done. They can both complain about the problem, but one person might get the brush-off while the other one gets an apology or a refund.

It often comes down to that old expression, "You can catch more flies with honey than vinegar." As parents and teachers have probably told you, being polite pays off. Using the sweet approach (honey) is usually more effective than using the sour approach (vinegar).

Here's how it works. Say you see an ad for a new soda pop on TV. In trying to get a laugh, the ad makes fun of a person with a foreign accent.

You think the ad is mean-spirited and unfair, that it encourages kids to pick on someone who's different. Instead of just concentrating on your own anger, you have to approach the advertiser in a way that ensures the company will take you seriously. In the message that you write to the TV station and to the soda company, you'll want to point out that:

1 You watch and like the TV station. This tells the station that you are part of their regular audience, and reminds them that they rely on your attention in order to attract advertisers.

2 You drink soda. This tells the advertiser that you are exactly the kind of person they're trying to persuade to try the new drink.

3 You are offended by the commercial. Here you'll want to explain what you don't like about the ad in a calm and clear manner. The more polite and reasonable you sound, the more likely they are to pay attention to your feedback.

4 You won't buy the soda as long as they air this ad. You're exercising your "Consumer Power" in a way that tells them the ad is backfiring.

5 You'll consider boycotting the TV station if the ad continues, which means you won't hear any of their other customers' ads, either!

6 You're planning to encourage friends and family to follow your lead, and to post your complaint on a social media site. This shows that you can gather together some "Companion Power," too.

7 You'd like a written response from both the TV station and the advertiser demonstrating that they understand your concerns, and telling you how they're going to act. This request will make it more difficult for them to ignore your letter. And if they have to go to the trouble of writing a response, they'll have to either figure out a way to defend their ad, or make a commitment to pulling it off the air.

Finally, when you sign the letter, you might also consider telling the station and the company how old you are. Because not very many young people write to companies, adding your age will make it easier for your letter to get noticed.

It's always a good idea to send your letter to both the advertiser and to its media "host"—the TV or radio station, website, mobile phone service, magazine or newspaper, billboard company, or bus line—that allowed the ad to be seen or heard in the first place. And you might also send your letter to the organization in your country in charge of advertising rules (see the resources at the back of the book).

~~DON'T~~ TRY THIS AT HOME!

Patent medicines that claimed they could cure everything from headaches to stomach ulcers were banned decades ago. And yet some advertisers still make promises that sound pretty unbelievable. If you see an ad that makes a claim you think sounds fishy, you can contact the company to ask for proof. Be clear that you're looking for evidence that's been gathered in a scientific way. And make sure you tell them you don't simply want more advertising. Sometimes people making such requests receive a whole whack of promotional brochures—in other words, more claims!—instead of actual proof.

ADVERTISING IMPACT: THE BIG PICTURE

The impact of advertising is much bigger than whether or not any one message persuades us to buy this product instead of that one. Because we're surrounded by so many sales messages all the time, we end up thinking about "things" and "shopping" more than we naturally would otherwise.

Imagine you're on a camping holiday with your family, far away from TV, internet, cell phone service, billboards, and magazines. Chances are you're too busy swimming or building a fire or putting up the tent to think about new products you just have to have. In fact, people who have lived or traveled in foreign countries where there's very little advertising say that it's a big shock when they come back to North America and see how much space ads take up here.

There are all sorts of really important things in life that don't advertise. But because ads don't normally deliver messages designed to remind us of how much pleasure we get from the stuff that *can't* be bought at a shopping mall, we probably spend less time striving for and valuing the things that really translate into more fun or a better world.

Some people are very concerned about how successful advertising has been in shifting our focus away from making and using what we need and toward buying more and more stuff simply because we can. Environmentalists point out that making, promoting, and buying products and then throwing them away uses up the Earth's resources. They remind us—sometimes in ads of their own—that there's a limited supply of clean air and water, wood, metal, oil, and gas. And they argue that lifestyles that require us to keep buying new things all the time make it harder for the planet to continue to support us.

AD-FREE CITY

In 2007, São Paolo, a city in Brazil, banned all outdoor advertisements, including billboards, ads on buses and taxis, and even signage on storefronts. Do you think banning all outdoor advertisements would make your city or town look better? Or do you think ads contribute to the color and character of a city? Can you imagine what Times Square in New York City would look like without any advertising?

STEP AWAY FROM THE MALL!

Originally, *Adbusters* was just a magazine; now it's a movement, too. Many people who embrace *Adbusters*' criticism of advertising and consumption call themselves "culture jammers." They create images of their own and spoof ads to encourage others to question the way in which our promotion-oriented culture affects how we think and behave. For instance, every year at the end of November—at the height of the Christmas shopping season—they promote "Buy Nothing Day." The point is to get people to stop and think about how much stuff we buy that we don't really need. Do you think this sort of campaign can make a difference in changing people's attitudes and shopping habits?

JUNK MAIL UNLIMITED

Have you ever taken stock of just how many flyers, catalogs, coupons, and contest promotions find their way into your home every day? One estimate suggests that bulk mail destroys more than 60 million trees a year and creates 4 million tons of waste. In order to avoid contributing to this process, many people are now putting signs on their mailboxes saying "No Junk Mail" or signing up for "Do Not Contact" lists.

THERE IS NO "AWAY"

Do you ever think about what happens when you toss out an old toy or T-shirt because it's broken or you've outgrown it? When we throw things away, where exactly IS "away"? More and more, people are realizing that although the world seems awfully big, it's actually quite small. And so far, no one's invented an interplanetary disposal service.

Imagine you just got a new cell phone, and now you've decided you might as well trash your old one because it's an ancient model and some of the keys stick anyway. Without even getting into the merits of recycling electronics versus throwing them away, let's look at the mountain of stuff that had to be used up or thrown out even before the phone existed:

I EXTRACTING RESOURCES: To make the phone, its plastic case and charger, the paper user's manual, and the cardboard box it came in, raw materials had to be mined and trees had to be cut down.

2 MANUFACTURING PRODUCTS: To transform the raw resources into electronic parts, plastic, paper, and cardboard, factories (which use lots of energy) had to be activated to pulp wood into cardboard and paper products and manufacture the plastic and metal parts. And guess what? Many of these processes created pollution and contaminated water.

3 ATTRACTING CUSTOMERS: To promote the phone, advertising campaigns were created, using more paper (for posters, magazine ads, and billboards), more resources in the form of film or optical discs (for TV commercials and movie trailers), and more energy (for electronic ads, and for the production of all of the above).

And this mountain of eventual waste was created before anyone bought the phone, and well before you decided to throw it "away"!

ADVERTISING FOR GOOD?

On the other hand, advertising is also used by people who are trying to *save* the environment. Organizations like Greenpeace, Ecojustice, and the World Wildlife Federation have developed billboard, print, web, and TV campaigns to encourage people to think about the impact their buying behavior has on our air, water, forests, and endangered animals.

Other advertising isn't about convincing people to consume, but about getting them to give. You've probably seen many ads for charities that raise money to help cure diseases, fight poverty, or support social causes. The ads are meant to raise awareness about specific issues and encourage people to donate money to the causes. In fact, there are some advertising agencies that will only accept clients who are promoting a worthwhile social cause, rather than selling a product.

SHOCK TACTICS

Sometimes charities use upsetting images in their ads to make a statement, like images of hungry children or disease victims. And the more shocking ads are often the ones that go viral. But some people have objected to these campaigns, for trying to persuade people to give money by making them feel sad or guilty. Critics also argue that shock strategies can be effective at first, but after a while people who see the ad experience "compassion fatigue" and stop responding to the disturbing image.

If you saw an ad for a charity with an image of an abandoned animal or a sad child, would you be more likely to support the cause? Or would you feel like your emotions were being manipulated? Do unglamorous social problems need shocking ads to get people to pay attention?

AND THEY SAID IT COULDN'T BE DONE!

The wholesale chain store Costco sells nearly $100 *billion* worth of groceries and merchandise every year. Most companies of that size would have an advertising budget over $100 million. Yet Costco spends almost nothing on advertising, and doesn't even have public relations staff. Instead, it promotes itself through word of mouth, and by building good relationships with its customers (who even pay a membership fee to shop at the store!). Costco has also earned good press for its environmentally and socially responsible practices. And it has been able to pass along some of its savings from not advertising by offering lower prices to customers, and higher salaries and benefits to employees.

Many marketing experts claim that a business can't remain successful if it doesn't advertise. They say that it doesn't matter how good a company's products are; if the company doesn't buy time on TV or space in magazines or on websites, then no one will buy what it's selling. But Costco, and other companies like The Body Shop and Lululemon that don't rely on traditional advertising, have proven those experts wrong.

What do you think of the no-ads approach? Do you think it could work for other products, such as movies and games?

AND THE AWARD GOES TO...

Advertising can be an art. After all, it is hard to get people's attention, make them laugh or cry, and still remember what you're trying to sell. So, just like the Academy Awards, there are awards that celebrate the creativity of clever advertising campaigns. At the Cannes Lions International Festival of Creativity, advertisements from all over the world are submitted for judging. In 2012, there were over 34,000 entries! Can you imagine being a judge for that contest?

AD EXECS:
THE NEXT GENERATION

Years from now, many kids from your generation will be working in advertising or related fields. Some will have jobs researching, thinking up, writing, shooting, designing, directing, or acting in commercials. And some will be making decisions about how to promote a company's product or service. You'll have the opportunity to change what you don't like about advertising by doing things differently. You might even choose NOT to advertise!

CAREERS IN ADVERTISING

It takes a village to create an ad. Most originate in ad agencies, which are hired by companies to develop advertising campaigns. A typical ad agency features the following kinds of people:

CREATIVE STAFF

includes copywriters and art directors, who work in teams to come up with creative ideas. Copywriters write the slogans or other text, while art directors are responsible for planning the visuals.

ACCOUNT EXECUTIVES

represent the clients (companies) at the agency, and make sure the ad campaigns meets the companies' needs.

PRODUCTION STAFF

ensure the ad actually gets made. They contact directors and production companies to film TV commercials, or photographers, designers, artists, and printers to create print ads.

MEDIA BUYERS

are responsible for placing the finished ads where they will have the most impact. They advise clients whether to buy commercial time on TV or radio, ad space in magazines or newspapers, or promote their products on websites, bus shelters or billboards.

MAKE YOUR OWN AD!

After all this reading and thinking about advertising, do you feel like an expert? Now that you understand its persuasive power, you may want to experiment with advertising yourself. Maybe you're on student council and want people to come to the spring dance. Or maybe your family wants to clear out the basement and decides to have a garage sale. To get the word out, you're going to need to put some advertising techniques to work!

START BY ASKING YOURSELF A FEW QUESTIONS:

- What are you selling? Is it a product or an event?

- Who are you selling it to? What's the best way to reach those people?

- What does your product do? Why will people need or want it?

- What is the most appealing thing about your product?

ONCE YOU HAVE AN IDEA OF WHAT YOU WANT TO SAY WITH YOUR AD, GET TO WORK:

- Start early: if you're planning an event, like a garage sale or a dance, you don't want to leave advertising until the last minute.

- Come up with a slogan, keeping it short and sweet—you should have one line that sums up the message you want people to remember.

- Know your audience: different people respond to ads differently, so make sure you think about who you're targeting, and develop your ads to appeal to them. This might mean making different ads to reach different types of customers, or advertising in more than one place (for instance, posting on Facebook as well as putting up printed posters).

- Match your images to your message: Adding computer graphics, photos, or illustrations can make your ad more interesting to look at. If you want to use somebody else's illustration or photo, make sure you get permission first.

- Make sure the ad includes all the relevant information, or a way for people to get that information (such as a link to a website, or an email address or phone number).

- Follow the Z: Some people say that in North America we scan pages, both print and electronic, in a Z fashion—across the top from left to right, on a diagonal from the right top corner to the left bottom corner, then left to right across the bottom. Why does this matter? You'll want to put all your most important information along these lines so that people scanning your ad get all the details they need.

- Make sure that you get someone else to look at your ad before you make copies of it or post it on the internet. A second (or third, or fourth) opinion is always useful, in case something that makes sense to you is unclear to someone else. They can also watch for spelling mistakes!

PASS YOUR OWN TEST

As the old proverb from chapter 1—"To the fish, the water is invisible"—reminds us, advertising is an inescapable part of life in North America. We're basically swimming in commercial messages everywhere we go. And it's really important to be as aware as possible of the kind of "water" surrounding us. Informed swimmers remember to ask themselves:

Who wants me to believe this?

How do they benefit if I do?

What ELSE does this ad sell?

What does the ad leave out?

AD RESOURCES

Want to exercise your Complaint Power or stay informed about advertising issues? The following organizations can help.

UNITED STATES	CANADA
Government Regulators	
Federal Trade Commission (FTC): www.ftc.gov

This government organization enforces US laws—including those relating to advertising practice—that are designed to protect consumers. | The Canadian Radio-Television and Telecommunications Commission (CRTC): www.crtc.gc.ca

The CRTC is an independent agency that regulates Canadian broadcasting and telecommunication systems. |
| **Industry Organizations** | |
| Children's Advertising Review Unit (CARU): www.asrcreviews.org

CARU reviews advertising and promotional material directed at children in all media, encouraging advertisers to adhere to the Self-Regulatory Guidelines for Children's Advertising. | Advertising Standards Canada (ASC): www.adstandards.com

This industry organization handles consumer complaints about Canadian advertising and encourages advertisers to follow the voluntary rules. |

Consumer Organizations

National Institute for Media and the Family:
www.parentfurther.com/technology-media

This nonprofit organization is a national resource for research, education, and information about the impact of media on children and families. It works to increase the benefits and reduce the harm of media.

MediaSmarts:
www.mediasmarts.ca

The network's comprehensive website promotes and supports media education in Canadian schools, homes, and communities. It promotes debate about the impact of media in people's lives, encourages critical thinking about media, and features games and activities for young people.

MediaWatch:
www.mediawatch.com

This national nonprofit women's organization promotes the improved portrayal and representation of women and girls in the media through research, education, and lobbying.

Adbusters Media Foundation:
www.adbusters.org

The Adbusters Media Foundation is a global network of artists, activists, writers, pranksters, students, educators, and entrepreneurs. It operates a website and publishes *Adbusters* magazine, which critiques the advertising industry, promotional culture, and consumerism.

NOTES

CHAPTER 1

Babylonia; ancient Greece; early Rome. Frank Presbrey. *The History and Development of Advertising*. New York: Greenwood Press, 1968, 4–14.

shingle signs. Benjamin D. Singer. *Advertising and Society*. 2nd ed. Toronto: Captus Press, 1994, 17.

street carts; newspaper ads. Stephen Kline. *Out of the Garden*. Toronto: Garamond Press, 1993, 27.

printing press to photography. Courtland L. Bovee. *Contemporary Advertising*. New York: McGraw-Hill, 1994.

patent medicines. Steven Fox. *The Mirror Makers: A History of American Advertising and Its Creators*. New York: William Morrow & Co., 1984, 16–18.

Coca-Cola sidebar. Greg Myers. *Adworlds: Brands, Media Audiences*. London: Arnold, 1999. Also at www.colafountain.co.uk

Kraft Television Theatre. The Museum of Broadcast Communications. www.museum.tv/archives/etv/K/htmlK/krafttelevis/krafttelevis.htm

logos. Ellen Lupton and J. Abbott Miller. *Design Writing Research: Writing on Graphic Design*. New York: Kiosk, 1996, 177.

"advertising chatter"; products sold on radio and TV. W. Leiss, S. Kline, S. Jhally. *Social Communication in Advertising*. Toronto: University of Toronto Press, 1986, 104–12.

modern TV advertising strategies. Candace Lombardi. "TV Advertising's DVR Challenge." *CNet News*, May 23, 2006. Retrieved May 30, 2012, from http://news.cnet.com/TV-advertisings-DVR-challenge/2100-1024_3-6075233.html

in-game advertising. Owen Good. "President Obama Returns to *Madden*—Through In-Game Advertising." *Kotaku*, Sept. 14, 2012. Retrieved May 31, 2012, from http://kotaku.com/5943462/president-obama-returns-to-madden++through-in+game-advertising. Also Jenni Lada. "Metal Gear Solid: Peace Walker sold out (and not in a good way)." *Technology Tell*, April 7, 2010. Retrieved May 31, 2012, from http://www.technologytell.com/gaming/55395/metal-gear-solid-peace-walker-sold-out-and-not-in-a-good-way/

Star Wars commercial tie-ins. Mayrav Saar and Olivia Hawkinson. *The Orange County Register*, May 17, 1999.

CHAPTER 2

nag factor. "Kids learn early to nag, study finds." *The Vancouver Sun*, June 18, 2002.

back-seat customers. Nancy Day. *Advertising: Information or Manipulation?* Berkely Heights, NJ: Enslow Publishers, 1999.

"Scream Until Dad Stops." Selina S. Guber and Jon Berry. *Marketing To and Through Kids*. New York: McGraw-Hill, 1993.

cookies. "How Advertisers Use Internet Cookies to Track You" (video). *WSJ Live*, July 30, 2010. Retrieved June 6, 2012, from http://live.wsj.com/video/how-advertisers-use-internet-cookies-to-track-you/92E525EB-9E4A-4399-817D-8C4E6EF68F93.html#!92E525EB-9E4A-4399-817D-8C4E6EF68F93

children disproportionately targeted by online ads. "Children 'targeted' by online advertisements" (video). BBC News website, Jan. 31, 2011. Retrieved June 6, 2012, from http://news.bbc.co.uk/2/hi/programmes/click_online/9379674.stm. Also Steve Stecklow. "On the Web, Children Face Intensive Tracking." *The Wall Street Journal*, Sept. 17, 2010. Retrieved June 6, 2012, from http://online.wsj.com/article/SB10001424052748703904304575497903523187146.html

fast food marketing. Fast Food FACTS website. www.fastfoodmarketing.org. Retrieved Sept. 20, 2012.

ads on school lockers. Sue Shellenbarger. "Should Ads be Allowed in Schools?" *The Wall Street Journal*, Jan. 6, 2011. Retrieved June 7, 2012, from http://blogs.wsj.com/juggle/2011/01/06/should-ads-be-allowed-in-schools/

Channel One. Channel One News website. www.channelone.com. Retrieved June 7, 2012.

research on impact of Channel One. Roy F. Fox. "How Channel One's TV Commercials Affect Students' Thinking, Language, Behavior." Testimony to US Senate Hearing on Channel One, May 20, 1999. Retrieved from www.commercialalert.org

toothpaste drills and cocoa demonstrations. Stuart Ewen. *Captains of Consciousness*. New York: McGraw-Hill, 1976, 90.

Coke day at high school in Evans, GA. "Coke Day prank fizzles for Pepsi-loving student." Assoc. Press article in various papers, including *Hannibal Courier-Post,* March 26, 1998.

third-person effect. W. P. Davidson. "The third-person effect in communication." *Public Opinion Quarterly 47,* 1983, 1–15.

research about preschoolers. R. M. Liebert and J. Sprafkin. *The Early Window.* New York: Pergamon, 1988.

stages of cognition in child development. Anne Sutherland and Beth Thompson. *Kidfluence: Why Kids Today Mean Business.* New York: McGraw-Hill Ryerson, 2001.

effects of advertising on teens. Agnes Nairn. "Changing the Rules of the Game: Implicit Persuasion and Interactive Children's Marketing." Retrieved June 15, 2012, from http://changelabsolutions.org/sites/default/files/documents/Implicit_persuasion_in_interactive_marketing.pdf

words used to advertise girls' and boys' toys. Crystal Smith. "Word Cloud: How Toy Ad Vocabulary Reinforces Gender Stereotypes." *The Achilles Effect.* Retrieved Feb. 13, 2013, from http://www.achilleseffect.com/2011/03/word-cloud-how-toy-ad-vocabulary-reinforces-gender-stereotypes/#

CHAPTER 3

tracking ad success. Kashmir Hill. "Facebook Is Tracking What Users Buy In Stores To See Whether Its Ads Work." *Forbes* website, Sept. 26, 2012. Retrieved Oct. 1, 2012, from http://www.forbes.com/sites/kashmirhill/2012/09/26/facebook-is-tracking-what-users-buy-in-stores-to-see-whether-its-ads-work/

banner blindness. Magnus Pagendarm and Heike Schaumburg. "Why Are Users Banner-Blind? The Impact of Navigation Style on the Perception of Web Banners." *Journal of Digital Information*, Feb. 2, 2006. Retrieved Oct. 1, 2012, from http://journals.tdl.org/jodi/index.php/jodi/article/view/36/38

t-commerce. Trefis Team. "Is TV-Commerce PayPal's Next Big Opportunity?" *Forbes* website, June 21, 2012. Retrieved Oct. 1, 2012, from http://www.forbes.com/sites/greatspeculations/2012/06/21/is-tv-commerce-paypals-next-big-opportunity/. Also Delivery Agent website, www.deliveryagent.com

stereotypes in advertising. "Visible Minorities in Entertainment Media." *Media Smarts*. Retrieved Oct. 3, 2012, from http://mediasmarts.ca/diversity-media/visible-minorities/visible-minorities-entertainment-media

DVRs and ad skipping. Shalini Ramachandran. "Zap! New DVR Wipes Out Ads." *The Wall Street Journal*, May 11, 2012. Retrieved Oct. 8, 2012, from http://online.wsj.com/article/SB10001424052702304070304577396470142982532.html

ads without words. Alex Benady. "The Death of Dialogue." *Campaign*, Oct. 17, 2008. Retrieved Oct. 8, 2012, from http://www.campaignlive.co.uk/features/854999/

"Biggie" campaign. Lisa R. Young and Marion Nestle. "Portion Sizes and Obesity: Responses of Fast-Food Companies." *Journal of Public Health Policy* 28 (July 1, 2007): 238–48.

headache remedy. D. Bem. *Beliefs, Attitudes, and Human Affairs*. Belmont, CA: Brooks/Cole, 1970.

greenwashing. "10 Worst Household Products for Greenwashing." CBC News website, Sept. 14, 2012. Retrieved Oct. 10, 2012, from http://www.cbc.ca/news/canada/story/2012/09/14/greenwashing-labels-marketplace.html. Also Greenwashing Index website. www.greenwashingindex.com

cost of Super Bowl commercials. www.superbowl.com

between 20% and 40% of price of product. Shelagh Wallace. *The TV Book: Talking Back to Your TV*. Toronto: Annick Press, 1998, 56.

impact of repetition. Anthony Pratkanis and Elliot Aronson. *Age of Propaganda: The Everyday Use and Abuse of Persuasion*. New York: W. H. Freemand & Co., 2001, 181–82.

food that looks too good to eat. www.zillions.org (website no longer exists).

Photoshop backlash. Jim Edwards. "US Moves Toward Banning Photoshop In Cosmetics Ads." Business Insider (website), Dec. 16, 2011. Retrieved Oct. 15, 2012, from http://articles.businessinsider.com/2011-12-16/news/30523807_1_nad-advertising-standards-authority-misleading-ads

Dove campaign. http://www.dove.us/Social-Mission/campaign-for-real-beauty.aspx. Retrieved Oct. 15, 2012.

CHAPTER 4

guerilla marketing. Terry O'Reilly and Mike Tennant. *The Age of Persuasion*. Toronto: Knopf, 2009, 123–24. Also Ryan Lum. "122 Must See Guerilla Marketing Examples." Retrieved Nov. 5, 2012, from http://www.creativeguerrillamarketing.com/guerrilla-marketing/122-must-see-guerilla-marketing-examples/

Happiness Machine. Sheila Shayon. "Coca-Cola Continues to Open Happiness, From Coke Machine to Truck to Table." *Brandchannel*. Retrieved Nov. 5, 2012, from http://www.brandchannel.com/home/post/2012/09/19/Coca-Cola-Open-Happiness-091912.aspx

Sony Ericsson Mobile phone/camera, guerrilla marketing. Suzanne Vranica. "Sony Ericsson campaign uses actors to push cameraphone in real life." *The Wall Street Journal*, July 31, 2002.

paid product reviews. David Streitfeld. "The Best Book Reviews Money Can Buy." *The New York Times*, August 25, 2012. Retrieved Nov. 5, 2012, from http://www.nytimes.com/2012/08/26/business/book-reviewers-for-hire-meet-a-demand-for-online-raves.html?_r=5&pagewanted=all&

cool hunt. Malcolm Gladwell. "The Coolhunt." *The New Yorker*, March 17, 1997.

E.T./Reese's Pieces. Tom Brook. "Hollywood for sale." BBC News website, Nov. 25, 2000. http://news.bbc.co.uk/1/hi/entertainment/1039137.stm

movie product placements. Dale Buss. "A product placement hall of fame." Business Week Online, June 22, 1998. www.businessweek.com/1998/25/b3583062.htm

Apple and product placement. Tiffany Kaiser. "Apple Gets Free Product Placement in TV Shows, Movies." *DailyTech*, May 14, 2012. Retrieved Nov. 7, 2012, from http://www.dailytech.com/article.aspx?newsid=24679. Also Abe Sauer. "Announcing the Brandcameo Product Placement Award Winners." *Brandchannel*, Feb. 22, 2011. Retrieved Nov. 7, 2012, from http://www.brandchannel.com/home/post/2011/02/22/2010-Brandcameo-Product-Placement-Awards.aspx

Transformers. "Product Placement in Movies: A Brief History." *MirriAd* , Jan. 17, 2012. Retrieved Nov. 7, 2012, from http://www.mirriad.com/2012/01/product-placement-in-movies-a-brief-history/

TV show placements. Peter Vamos. "Branded content: Good for the goose and the gander." *Playback Magazine,* May 27, 2002. Also "Primetime Shows With the Most Product Placement." CNBC website. Retrieved Nov. 7, 2012, from http://www.cnbc.com/id/45884892/Primetime_Shows_With_the_ Most_Product_Placement?slide=5

Walmart and Procter & Gamble. "Walmart and Procter & Gamble Collaborate to Provide Family-Friendly TV Programming." Walmart website. Retrieved Nov. 7, 2012, from http://news.walmart. com/news-archive/2010/02/10/walmart-procter-gamble-collaborate-to-provide-family-friendly-tv-programming

subliminal ads. Bob Garfield. "Perspective: 'Subliminal' seduction, and other urban myths." *Advertising Age,* Sept. 14, 2000. www.adage.com/news.cms?newsId=32008

program-length ads on Saturday morning cartoons. Stephen Kline. *Out of the Garden.* Toronto: Garamond Press, 1993, 218–30. Also in Ellen Seiter. *Sold Separately: Parents and Children in Consumer Culture.* New Brunswick, NJ: Rutgers University Press, 1993, 147–70.

cereal and candy books for toddlers. David D. Kilpatrick. "Snack foods become stars of books for children." *The New York Times,* Sept. 22, 2000.

advergames. Alice Park. "Can Online Games Influence What Kids Eat?" *Time,* Jan. 10, 2012. Retrieved Nov. 8, 2012, from http://healthland.time.com/2012/01/10/how-online-games-can-influence-what-kids-eat/

Rihanna example. Richard James. "Rihanna: The carefully marketed party girl who just wants you to notice her." Metro Blogs, Nov. 20, 2012. Retrieved Nov. 26, 2012, from http://blogs.metro.co.uk/music/rihanna-the-carefully-marketed-party-girl-just-wants-notice/

advertorials. Terri Thornton. "Revamped Forbes Pushes Advertorials, Social Media, Conflict." PBS MediaShift, Oct. 13, 2010. Retrieved Nov. 26, 2012, from http://www.pbs.org/mediashift/2010/10/revamped-forbes-pushes-advertorials-social-media-conflict286.html

advertisers' influence on magazine content. Gloria Steinem. "Sex, Lies and Advertising." *MS Magazine,* July/Aug. 1990.

CHAPTER 5

Scott Paper toilet paper, Listerine scare tactics. Roland Marchand. *Advertising the American Dream: Making Way for Modernity, 1920–1940.* Berkeley: University of California Press, 1985, 102–3.

Listerine apology. William E. Francois. *Mass Media Law and Regulation.* 4th ed. New York: John Wiley & Sons, 1986. citing *FTC News Summary,* Dec. 18, 1975.

regulations in European countries. Also in J. Weber. "Selling to kids: At what price?" *Boston Globe,* May 18, 1997.

self-regulatory guidelines for US advertisers. Children's Advertising Review Unit (CARU) of the Council of Better Business Bureaus Inc.; www.caru.org/guidelines

Canadian regulations. Advertising Standards Canada; www.adstandards.com

behavioral advertising. "Policy Position on Online Behavioural Advertising." Office of the Privacy Commissioner of Canada. Retrieved Dec. 3, 2012, from http://www.priv.gc.ca/information/guide/2012/bg_ba_1206_e.asp

response to Do Not Track proposals. Natasha Singer. "A Trail of Clicks, Culminating in Conflict." *The New York Times,* Nov. 5, 2012. Retrieved Dec. 3, 2012, from http://www.nytimes.com/2012/11/06/technology/silicon-valley-objects-to-online-privacy-rule-proposals-for-children.html?pagewanted=1&ref=onlineprivacyregulation. Also Natasha Singer. "Do Not Track? Advertisers Say 'Don't Tread on Us'" *The New York Times,* Oct. 13, 2012. Retrieved Dec. 3, 2012, from http://www.nytimes.com/2012/10/14/technology/do-not-track-movement-is-drawing-advertisers-fire.html?_r=0 credit cards and online advertising. Emily Steel. "Using Credit Cards to Target Web Ads." *The Wall Street Journal*, Oct. 25, 2011. Retrieved Dec. 3, 2012, from http://online.wsj.com/article/SB1000142405 2970204002304576627030651339352.html?mod=WSJ_whattheyknow2011_3UP

social advertising. "Social Advertising Best Practices." Interactive Advertising Bureau, 2009. Retrieved Dec. 3, 2012, from http://www.iab.net/media/file/Social-Advertising-Best-Practices-0509.pdf

spam. Tim Barker. "Experts say spam e-mail grows because it works." *Phys.Org*, Jan. 4, 2010. Retrieved Dec. 5, 2012, from http://phys.org/news181853790.html

It's Everywhere examples: Barbie Pink Month. Dan Chung. "Ash Street in Manchester painted pink for Barbie month." Reuters Toppix News and Sports, Nov. 11, 1997. Columbia Encyclopedia website at www.encyclopedia.com; Pepsi and Coke in Himalayas. "Court to fine companies for painting ads on Himalayas." Agence France-Presse. *The National Post*, Sept. 3, 2002.

Joe Camel. P. M. Fischer, M. P. Schwartz, J. W. Richards Jr., A. O. Goldstein and T. H. Rojas. "Brand logo recognition by children aged 3 to 6 years. *Journal of the American Medical Association*. vol. 245, no. 16, 1667–68. As cited in Kilbourne. *Deadly Persuasion*, 183.

regulators ban Joe Camel. J. M. Broder. "FTC Charges 'Joe Camel' ad illegally takes aim at minors." *The New York Times*. 29 May 1997.

Hollywood movies and the tobacco industry. Smoke Free Movies. A project of Stanton A. Glantz, Professor of Medicine at University of California, San Francisco. http://smokefreemovies.ucsf. edu/problem/fact_fiction.html. Also "Smoking in Movies Increases in 2011, Reverses Five Years of Progress." *Science Daily*, Sept. 27, 2012. Retrieved Dec. 6, 2012, from http://www.sciencedaily.com/ releases/2012/09/120927123646.htm

CHAPTER 6

complaint form adapted from MediaWatch website. www.mediawatch.ca

junk mail. No Junk Mail campaign. http://www.reddotcampaign.ca/

shock tactics in charity advertising. Regina Yau. "Why charities should abandon shock advertising." *The Guardian*, Aug. 30, 2012. Retrieved Dec. 10, 2012, from http://www.guardian.co.uk/ voluntary-sector-network/2012/aug/30/charities-should-abandon-shock-advertising

companies that don't advertise. Terry O'Reilly. "Great Brands Built Without Advertising." CBC radio, *Under the Influence*. Retrieved Dec. 10, 2012, from http://www.cbc.ca/undertheinfluence/ season-1/2012/01/28/great-brands-built-without-advertising/

Costco. Lori Gordon Logan and Michael Beyman. "Costco: Breaking All the Retail Rules." CNBC website, April 25, 2012. Retrieved Dec. 10, 2012, from http://www.cnbc.com/id/47175492

Cannes Lions International Festival of Creativity. http://www.canneslions.com/about/

jobs in advertising. Advertising Educational Foundation. http://www.aef.com/industry/ careers/9000#creative

INDEX

ACKNOWLEDGMENTS

My sincerest gratitude to Annick Press for recognizing the value and importance of a book about advertising for children in the first place, and for investing in its update in the second; to the thoughtful and creative Paula Ayer for her research and writing contributions to update the original book and incorporate additional dimensions and examples; to Michelle Lamoreaux for enlivening the pages with relevant cartoons; to Natalie Olsen for the engaging design; to Pamela Robertson, for providing wise and encouraging editing advice; to Amelia Izadpanah, Clea Sackville, Jocelyn Good, Sarah Hillworth, and Sophie Ploettel for sharing their perceptions and insights with such enthusiasm; to Andrea Smith and Kamran Izadpanah for suggesting and convening the focus group; to Shailen Vallabh for asking intelligent questions about the manuscript; to Drew Kelsall for providing speedy feedback; to the staff and board members of MediaWatch for their support and encouragement; to Stephen Kline and Simon Fraser University's School of Communication for enriching my own media education; and to David Mitchell, for pretty much everything else.

ABOUT THE AUTHOR

Growing up, Shari Graydon wasn't allowed to watch TV on school nights, so she read a lot of books. She didn't always appreciate it at the time, but now she's convinced it helped her to become a writer. Since then, Shari has written all kinds of things: brochures and newsletters for big companies and hospitals, chapters for textbooks, columns for newspapers, commentaries for radio, speeches for politicians, and even programs for television. She has taught media literacy at university and is a former president of the non-profit women's group MediaWatch, all of which helped her to write this book. She now lives in Ottawa, Ontario, where she runs a social enterprise called Informed Opinions and trains expert women to translate their knowledge into accessible commentary.

ABOUT THE ILLUSTRATOR

Michelle Lamoreaux is an illustrator from southern Utah. She works with many publishers, agencies, and magazines throughout the US. She currently lives in Salt Lake City.

LOOK FOR THESE OTHER GREAT BOOKS FROM ANNICK PRESS:

Attack of the Killer Video Book, Take Two
Tips and Tricks for Young Directors,
Revised and Updated
by Mark Shulman and Hazlitt Krog
illustrated by Martha Newbigging
PAPERBACK $14.95 | HARDCOVER $24.95

"This is a terrific book ... buy a couple of copies ... in case one goes missing in action. It's that good." —*CM Reviews*

"... offers the latest tips for young filmmakers ... a very kid-friendly handbook." —Reading Today Online

"... for children and teens who want to know the basics, this book will be a perfect place to start." —keenreaders.org

Nibbling on Einstein's Brain
Revised Edition
The Good, the Bad, and the Bogus in Science
by Diane Swanson
illustrated by Francis Blake
PAPERBACK $12.95 | HARDCOVER $24.95

Winner of numerous awards and accolades, including:
* Booklist's Top 10 Sci-Tech Books for Youth, 2002
* VOYA's Non-Fiction Honor List, 2002
* White Raven Collection, International Youth Library, Munich, 2002
* Eisenhower Collection of Math and Science Books, 2002
* Best Books, Canadian Children's Book Centre, 2010